★ Our Plan for America ★
STRONGER AT HOME, RESPECTED IN THE WORLD

Kerry Edwards
A STRONGER AMERICA

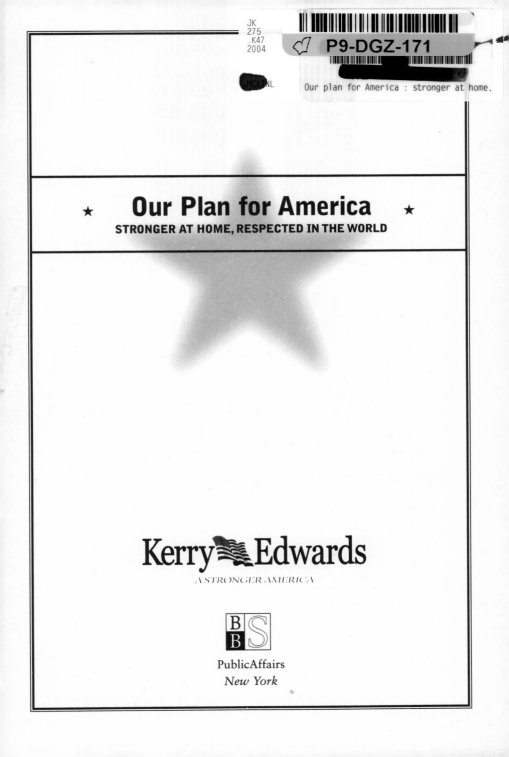

PublicAffairs
New York

Book Design by Polina Pinchevsky, NANA Design
ISBN 1–58648–314–5

First Edition
10 9 8 7 6 5 4 3 2 1

TABLE OF CONTENTS

★

★

Introduction

Our vision for America is a nation strong at home and respected in the world: strong at home because our families are strong and the promise of America is secure; respected in the world because our nation is strong and the promise of our example is restored. We are honored to offer America our vision and we are sure of the promise tomorrow holds for the country we love.

Today, our country faces challenges that are new and profound. We are fighting a global war against a diffuse and scattered enemy that has already attacked us at home for the first time in generations. The great American middle class, whose hard work and ingenuity built the strong America of the 20th century, is being squeezed by declining incomes and the staggering costs that families are facing in education, health care, and energy.

At its core, we believe the choice America faces in November comes down to two vastly different visions about how to meet those challenges.

President George Bush and Vice President Dick Cheney believe that more wealth for the most fortunate will somehow lead to success for everyone else. We believe that America always does best when all Americans have the opportunity to do well. They believe we can make America safe entirely on our own. We believe that we must never hesitate to defend our people, but that we can only truly be safe if we lead the world in a way that rallies support and commands respect.

They believe America is on the right course.

We believe it is time for a new direction.

This book is our plan to build an America that is stronger at home and respected in the world. We offer this plan because we believe this election should be about ideas to lift America up, not negative attacks that drag America down.

Our plan is rooted in our values: freedom, family, work; opportunity, equality, responsibility; love of country and faith.

It reflects certain unshakable principles: that all Americans deserve an equal chance to rise as high and go as far as their hard work and God-given talents can take them; that America's strength and security depend on our ability to be true to America's values—at home and abroad; that war should be the last resort, not the first, in the use of American power; and that government has a limited but essential role in American life, beginning with the safety of our people.

We believe in equal opportunity for all, but special privileges for none.

We believe the best measure of our nation's progress is the condition of America's great middle class.

We believe America's national security requires military strength, strong alliances, and homeland defense.

In this book, we present our plan to address a wide range of problems and opportunities the country will face over the next four years. But we strongly believe that four challenges are especially urgent: keeping America safe and strong; reviving the American economy and providing more opportunity for middle-class families; fixing our health care system by holding down costs and expanding access to coverage; and charting a path to energy independence.

Our plan is specific, it is realistic, and it is responsible.

It will reduce, not increase, the federal budget deficit.

It will expand opportunity, not the size of the federal government.

And our plan will not raise taxes for the middle class—it will cut taxes for 98 percent of individuals and 99 percent of companies.

We understand that people have grown skeptical of vague election-year promises. That is why we are offering specific plans that you can read and weigh. And we expect to be held accountable for them.

If our plan sounds too ambitious, we hope you will remember this: under the last Democratic administration, America succeeded in addressing big challenges. After thirty years of federal budget deficits, the budget was balanced and then produced a surplus. After thirty years of stagnant middle-class wages, real incomes rose dramatically, leading to the biggest expansion of the middle class since the 1960s. After a quarter century of rising violent crime rates, crime was cut dramatically year after year, making America's big cities safer than they had been in decades.

We have arrived here together from different places. Our lives are different stories; our struggles have left different scars; our triumphs tell different tales. But the things we believe are the values our parents taught us, and the lessons America gave—that freedom is sacred, and opportunity must be shared; that responsibility brings strength, and trust requires truth; that faith is a comfort, and service a blessing. And that in America, when we are true to our values and united in our cause, nothing in the world can stop us. There is nothing we cannot do.

John Kerry and John Edwards

Section One

★

Chapter One

SECURITY

America was born in pursuit

of an idea—that a free people

with diverse beliefs could govern

themselves in peace.

John Kerry

★

A Strong, Respected America

Government has no greater purpose than the security and welfare of its people. We stand ready to meet that responsibility with a plan to protect our people and safeguard our values; to build a stronger, safer America, once more respected throughout the world. We approach this task with gravity, humility, and resolve. Gravity, because the stakes are high. Humility, because the responsibility is great. And resolve, because we must prevail.

We offer a vision grounded in the tough-minded tradition of engagement and leadership that was forged by Wilson and Roosevelt in two World Wars, then championed by Truman and Kennedy during the Cold War. Our overriding goals are to protect our people and our way of life; and to help build a safer, more peaceful, more prosperous, more democratic world.

Alone among nations, America was born in pursuit of an idea—that a free people with diverse beliefs could govern themselves in peace. It is an idea that has changed the course of history and transformed the world, bringing hope and freedom to millions.

For more than a century, America has spared no effort to defend, encourage, and promote that idea around the world. Over and over, we have done it by exercising American leadership to forge powerful alliances—with longtime allies and reluctant friends, with nations already living in the light of democracy and with peoples struggling to join them.

The might of those alliances has been a driving force in the survival and success of freedom—in two World Wars, in the Cold War, in the Gulf War, and in Kosovo. America led instead of going it alone. We extended a hand, not a fist. We respected the world—and the world respected us.

Today, there is a powerful yearning around the world for an America that listens and leads again. An America that is respected, not just feared. We believe that respect is an indispensable mark of our nation's character—and an indispensable source of our nation's strength. And it is the indispensable bond of America's mighty alliances.

Unfortunately, the Bush administration has walked away from more than a hundred years of American leadership *in* the world and embraced a new—and dangerously ineffective—American disregard *for* the world.

They rushed to force before exhausting diplomacy. They bullied when they should have persuaded. They acted alone when they should have assembled a team. They hoped for the best when they should have prepared for the worst. Time and again, this administration has confused leadership with going it alone and engagement with compromise of principle—they fail to understand that real leadership means standing by your principles and rallying others to join you.

We believe in an America that people all around the world admire and look up to, because they know that we cherish not just our freedom, but theirs. Not just our democracy, but their hope for it. Not just our peace and security, but the world's. We believe in an America that cherishes freedom, safeguards our people, forges alliances, and commands respect. And that is the America we are going to build.

Today, we face three great challenges above all others: first, to win the global war against terror; second, to stop the spread of nuclear, biological, and chemical weapons; and third, to promote democracy, development, and freedom around the world, starting by winning the peace in Iraq.

To meet these challenges, we need a new national security policy guided by four new imperatives: first, America must launch and lead a new era of alliances for the post-9/11 world. Second, we must modernize the world's most powerful military to meet the new threats. Third, in addition to our military might, we must deploy all that is in America's arsenal—our diplomacy, our intelligence system, our economic power, and the appeal of our values and ideas. Fourth and finally, to secure our full independence and freedom, we must free America from its dangerous dependence on Mideast oil.

DEFEATING TERRORISM

Today, America is waging a war against a global terrorist movement committed to our destruction. The war against terror is not just a manhunt—we cannot rest until Osama bin Laden is captured or killed, but that day will only mark a victory in the war on terror, not its end. Terrorists like al Qaeda and its affiliates are unlike any adversary our nation has known. We face a global jihadist movement of many groups, from different sources, with separate agendas, but all committed to assaulting the United States and free and open societies around the globe. Despite his tough talk, President Bush's actions against terrorism have fallen far short. He still has no comprehensive strategy for victory. After allowing bin Laden to escape from our grasp at Tora Bora, he diverted crucial resources from the effort to destroy al Qaeda in Afghanistan to fight the war in Iraq. And his doctrine of unilateral preemption has driven away our allies and cost us the support of other nations.

We must put in place a strategy to win—an approach that recognizes the complexity of the challenge and uses all the tools at our disposal. We need to recognize that the path to victory in the war on terror will be found in the company of others, not walking alone. We will never, ever wait for a green light from abroad when our safety is at stake—but we will not alienate those whose support we should have, and must enlist, for ultimate victory.

Victory in the war on terror requires a combination of American determination and international cooperation, and:

★ *The ability and willingness to direct immediate, effective military action to capture or destroy terrorist groups and their leaders,*

★ *A massive strengthening in intelligence gathering, analysis, and coordination coupled with vigorous law enforcement,*

★ *A relentless effort to shut down the flow of terrorist funds,*

★ *A global effort to prevent weak and failed states that can become sanctuaries for terrorists,*

★ *A sustained effort to deny terrorists any more recruits by working for peace, promoting democracy, economic growth and development, and improved education, and by conducting effective public diplomacy.*

Defending our people.

We will always be prepared to use military force to defeat terrorists before they strike at us. We will ensure that the world's best fighting forces are trained and equipped to seek out and destroy terrorists and their networks, and effectively conduct the operations necessary to deny them sanctuary.

Improving intelligence and law enforcement capabilities.

The global nature of the terrorist threat demands that we have international cooperation in order to succeed. As powerful as we are, we cannot be everywhere and learn everything without assistance from our friends and allies. Al Qaeda alone is known to operate in more than 60 countries. We need the cooperation of intelligence and law enforcement agencies around the world to cast a global net for terrorists, infiltrate their cells, learn their plans, cut off their funds, and stop them before they can attack. We will strengthen the effectiveness of intelligence and law enforcement efforts around the world by forging

stronger international coalitions and enhancing cooperative relationships.

We will also enhance the capabilities of our own
intelligence services. From the failure to uncover the
September 11th plot to the deeply flawed reports about
Iraq's weapons of mass destruction, we have experienced
significant intelligence failures in recent years. It is time
for serious reform. This will require the kind of leadership that the president has not provided. We will
strengthen our intelligence capabilities so that we can
more effectively prevent another terrorist attack by:

★ *Restoring the credibility of our intelligence community
 by ensuring the basic integrity of the intelligence process.
 We will make certain that our intelligence agencies are
 protected from political pressures and operate in a
 culture of diversity of thought, dissent, and forceful
 challenging of assumptions,*

★ *Strengthening accountability and leadership by creating
 a true Director of National Intelligence, a cabinet-level
 position with the authority to manage and direct all of
 the components of the intelligence community, including
 personnel and budgets,*

★ *Maximizing coordination and integration by structuring
 the intelligence community around key threats like
 terrorism, weapons of mass destruction, and hostile
 countries, so that all available resources are brought to
 bear on addressing the most pressing threats,*

★ *Transforming our intelligence services to ensure that they have sufficient personnel with the skills, languages, training, and orientation needed to meet today's threats. We will make sure that the FBI is fully prepared to perform necessary counter-terrorism intelligence operations and strengthen our capabilities overseas, particularly our clandestine services, so that we have our own robust human intelligence network.*

Cutting off terrorist funds.

Terrorists need money to operate—without it, they cannot procure weapons, pay for travel, and move freely. Our plan includes decisive steps to cut off the flow of terrorist funds. We will:

★ *Impose tough financial sanctions against nations or banks that engage in money laundering or fail to act against it,*

★ *Strengthen our money laundering laws to prevent terrorists from using unregulated institutions to finance terror,*

★ *Launch a "name and shame" campaign against those that are financing terror, and shut out of the U.S. financial system those nations that fail to respond,*

★ *End the Bush administration's kid-glove approach to the supply and laundering of terrorist money in Saudi Arabia and demand that Riyadh shut down Saudi-based "charities" that help finance al Qaeda and other terrorist networks.*

Preventing Afghanistan and other nations from becoming terrorist havens.

The Bush administration has badly mishandled the aftermath of the war in Afghanistan. Our drive to topple the Taliban regime convincingly demonstrated the courage and skill of our troops, the value of powerful new technologies, and the particular importance of Special Forces units in defeating unconventional enemies in the most difficult terrain imaginable.

Unfortunately, we have not followed that military victory with a plan or the commitment to win the peace. Two years ago, President Bush promised a Marshall Plan to rebuild that country. Instead, he has all but turned away from Afghanistan, allowing it to become a forgotten front in the war on terror and once again a potential breeding ground for terrorists. We will move immediately to reverse the Bush administration's dangerous neglect of Afghanistan. And we will take swift measures to help the Karzai government secure the country. We will:

★ *Work to further expand NATO forces outside Kabul and make good on its pledge to send additional troops to provide security for national elections,*

★ *Identify and destroy any al Qaeda training sites,*

★ *Accelerate training for the Afghan army and police,*

★ *Accelerate and expand the program to disarm warlord militias and reintegrate them into mainstream society,*

★ *Address the burgeoning opium trade by doubling our counter-narcotics assistance to the Karzai government.*

Beyond Afghanistan, terrorist attacks from Saudi Arabia and Indonesia to Kenya, Morocco, and Turkey point to a widespread and widening network of terrorists targeting this country and our friends. Failed and failing states, such as Somalia, or countries with large areas of limited government control, such as the Philippines and Indonesia, need international help to close down terrorist havens.

Improving public diplomacy.

America needs a major initiative in public diplomacy to support the many voices of freedom in the Arab and Muslim world. To improve education for the next generation of Muslim youth, we need a cooperative international effort to compete with radical madrassas. Democracy will not take root overnight, but America should speed that day with a strategy that aims at breaking down the economic and cultural isolation of much of this region, and supports local efforts to promote democracy, trade, tolerance, and respect for human rights. We will:

★ *Undertake a major initiative in public diplomacy to advance our interests and support voices of freedom in the Arab and Muslim world,*

★ *Lead an international effort to build schools and social services institutions that can marginalize radical organizations,*

★ *Support human rights groups, independent media, and labor unions working to build democracy and civil society throughout the Arab and Muslim world,*

★ *Reward governments that work toward the spread of freedom and democracy in the region, not those that work against it.*

STRENGTHENING OUR MILITARY

We need a new military to meet the new threats of the 21st century. Today's American military is the best in the world, but tomorrow's military must be better still—stronger, faster, better armed, and never again stretched so thin.

We will send a clear message to every man and woman in our armed forces: We guarantee that you will always be the best-led, best-equipped, and most respected fighting force in the world. You will be armed with the right weapons, trained in the right skills, and fully prepared to win on the battlefield. You will never again be sent into harm's way without enough troops for the task, nor asked to fight a war without a plan to win the peace. And you will never be given assignments which have not been clearly defined and for which you are not professionally trained.

The Bush administration was right to call for the "transformation" of the military—unfortunately, their version of transformation neglected to consider that the dangers we face have also transformed. They were concerned with fighting classic conventional wars, instead of the asymmetrical threats we now face in Iraq, Afghanistan, and in the war against al Qaeda. To rise to the challenges we face, we must strengthen our military, including our Special Forces; improve our technology; renew our commitment to the brave men and women who serve our country, and their families; and respect the advice, wisdom, and experience of our professional military.

Expanding active duty personnel.

As a first step, we will expand America's active duty forces. The war in Iraq has taken a real toll on our armed services. The vast majority of the Army's active duty combat divisions are committed to Iraq, either currently there, preparing to go, or recently returned.

To pick up the slack, we've called up our Guard and Reserves at historic levels. Some have been on the ground in Iraq for as many as 15 months—much longer than was expected or promised. And many of these units are being pushed to the limit, stretched far too thin. The administration's answer has just been to stretch further. They have extended tours of duty, delayed retirements, and prevented enlisted personnel from leaving the service—effectively using a stop-loss policy and the Individual Ready Reserve call-up as a back-door draft.

We need to expand the number of active duty soldiers, not to increase the number of soldiers in Iraq, but to sustain our overseas deployments and prevent and prepare for other possible conflicts. This will help relieve the strain on our troops and bring more of our soldiers, guardsmen, and reservists already serving abroad back home to their families. We also need to increase our capabilities in several areas, including: Special Forces, the troops who land behind enemy lines,

conduct counter-terrorism operations, perform reconnaissance missions, and gather intelligence; civil affairs
troops, those who work with local leaders and officials
to get schools back in shape, hospitals reopened, and
banks up and running; and military police, experts in
securing public order. We will:

★ *Expand America's active duty forces by 40,000,*

★ *Double the Army's Special Forces capability within
four years, while adding a special operations helicopter
squadron to the Air Force,*

★ *Increase by 50 percent the number of civil affairs troops
trained in the special responsibilities of post-conflict
reconstruction,*

★ *Increase our military police, because public order is
critical to establishing the conditions that allow peace
to take hold,*

★ *Add 500 "psychological operations" personnel and
augment their language training.*

Modernizing our military.

We cannot have a 21st century military unless we are
using 21st century technology and preparing our forces
for 21st century threats. That means educating, training,
and arming every soldier with state-of-the-art equipment,
whether it is body armor or weapons. And it means
employing the most sophisticated communications to
help our troops prevail and protect themselves in battle.
Right now, the technology exists to let a soldier see what

is over the next hill or around the next bend in the road. Every soldier in every unit should have access to that technology because it can mean the difference between life and death. And we will see to it that they do.

The Bush administration talks about military transformation, and takes credit for modernization efforts that were actually undertaken by the Clinton administration. Our troops need more than talk. We need a practical and specific plan for making our forces stronger by making them smarter. We offer a military modernization plan that will:

★ *Create more fully modernized "digital divisions," equipped with the latest communications technology crucial to future military success,*

★ *Create new "anti-proliferation" units trained and equipped to find and destroy nuclear, chemical and biological weapons, and to secure the facilities that produce them,*

★ *Provide full support for 21st century education and training for our troops, including training in how to deal effectively with culturally diverse civilian populations.*

We will also focus defense dollars on investing in the right technologies, including:

★ *Advanced communications and information technologies, to give our troops a crucial advantage in situational awareness and coordinating operations,*

★ *Sensing and control technologies, including robotic systems that minimize the risk of casualties,*

★ *Precision weapons, including "directed energy" weapons that can incapacitate the enemy, without risking the lives of innocent bystanders, for use in areas with large civilian populations.*

Standing up for military families.

We have an ironclad commitment to the men and women of our armed forces and their families. We will enact a Military Family Bill of Rights to ensure that our men and women in uniform and their families receive the benefits and respect they deserve. That includes:

★ *A commitment to full, mandatory funding of veterans' health care,*

★ *A commitment to competitive pay for service members, including special compensations for those in combat zones, such as family separation allowances and hazardous duty pay,*

★ *Up-to-date and accurate notice to military families about deployments and rotations that send troops away from home or back home,*

★ *Financial help for families affected by extended deployments,*

★ *A guarantee of adequate housing for military families, beginning with the accelerated construction by private developers of new housing on or near military bases,*

★ *Full access for all military personnel, whether active duty, National Guard, or Reserves, to TRICARE, the Defense Department's health care system,*

★ *Full funding for Department of Defense schools serving military families, which the Bush administration has sought to cut,*

★ *A new $250,000 gratuity for families of service members killed in a combat zone,*

★ *Doubling the period during which families of service members killed in action can continue to live in military housing.*

Keeping our Promise to American Veterans.

America entered into a covenant with those it drafted and those who enlisted, but the truth is, with every story of a veteran who goes without quality health care, housing, and a quality education, that covenant is broken. There are countless veterans who fought our wars who are now fighting year after year for the benefits they earned. Time and again the Bush administration has broken our nation's promise to our veterans.

★ *The Bush administration refuses to fully fund veterans' health care,*

★ *While boasting of cutting waitlists for VA health care, the Bush administration has done so by excluding nearly 500,000 veterans from enrolling,*

★ *The Bush administration has strongly opposed granting our nation's veterans full disability and retirement pay.*

We will end the game of playing politics with funding for veterans health care by making it mandatory. And we will end the "disabled veterans tax," under which military retirees who receive both veteran's pensions and disability compensation must surrender a dollar from their military retirement pay for every dollar they get for military compensation.

America deserves a commander-in-chief who will fight for a constant standard of decency and respect for those who serve their country in our armed forces—on active duty and as veterans. It should be no other way and in our administration, it will be no other way.

Making better use of the National Guard.

Finally, we need to make better use of what should be a key asset in homeland defense—our National Guard. The National Guard has served in every war, and they are serving now. They were the first ones called on to line city streets, guard bridges, and patrol our airports after September 11th. We will make homeland security one of their primary missions, and assign Guard units to a standing national task force on homeland security commanded by a National Guard general.

KEEPING WEAPONS OF MASS DESTRUCTION OUT OF THE HANDS OF TERRORISTS

There is no greater threat to American security than the possibility that a terrorist could acquire a chemical, biological, or nuclear weapon. Preventing terrorists from gaining access to weapons of mass destruction must be our number one security goal.

Defeating this massive threat requires American leadership of the highest order—leadership that brings our allies to greater collaboration, our friends to greater vigilance, our partners to greater participation. Unfortunately, the administration's policies have moved America in the opposite direction. They have weakened international agreements and initiatives instead of strengthening them. They have not done nearly enough to secure existing stockpiles and bomb-making materials. They have failed to take effective steps to stop the North Korean and Iranian nuclear programs. Our security requires an immediate change of course.

Defend America against attack at all costs.

First, the world should be on notice that we will take every possible measure to defend ourselves against the possibility of attack by unconventional arms. If such an attack appears imminent, we will do everything necessary to stop it. If such a strike does occur, we will respond with overwhelming and devastating force. We will do whatever is necessary to defend our country, and we will never cede our security to anyone. But we must not wait to act until we have no other choice but war. In this new world, we must deploy all the power in America's arsenal. We must build and lead an international consensus for early preventive action to lock up and secure existing weapons of mass destruction, and the material to manufacture more.

Secure and reduce existing nuclear weapons and material.

The first step is to safeguard all bomb-making material worldwide. We need to find it, catalog it, and lock it away. Our approach should be simple: treat the nuclear materials that make bombs like they are bombs. There is enough nuclear material to make literally thousands of nuclear weapons stored in inadequately protected sites all around the world. At the current pace, it will take 13 years to secure all the potential bomb material in the former Soviet Union alone. And the administration recently announced plans to remove bomb material from certain vulnerable sites outside the former Soviet Union over the next ten years. We cannot wait that long.

We cannot secure or destroy this material alone. International cooperation, especially with Russia and other states of the former Soviet Union, is absolutely necessary. This will be the highest possible priority in our administration, because there is no greater threat. We will:

★ *Make security of vulnerable nuclear material in the former Soviet Union a central issue in U.S.-Russian relations so that we can break through bureaucratic logjams and secure these dangerous materials within four years,*

★ *Complete a Global Cleanout by securing highly enriched uranium at research reactors in dozens of countries outside the former Soviet Union within four years,*

★ *Establish global standards for safeguarding nuclear materials and provide assistance, through expansion of the Cooperative Threat Reduction program, where necessary to help countries meet these standards,*

★ *Accelerate the timetable for joint U.S. and Russian reductions in nuclear arsenals,*

★ *Work with Russia to convert highly enriched uranium into energy reactor fuel, and to dispose of plutonium,*

★ *Lead by example, and end U.S. development of a new generation of nuclear weapons,*

★ *Work to reduce tension between India and Pakistan and guard against the possibility of their nuclear weapons falling into the wrong hands.*

End production of new fissile material for nuclear weapons.
Given the challenge of securing the thousands of nuclear weapons that already exist, the world does not need more nuclear weapons. There is strong international support for a ban on all production of highly enriched uranium and plutonium for use in nuclear weapons. We will immediately ask the members of the United Nations Security Council to formally pledge never again to produce such material for weapons. We will then lead a broad international coalition to verifiably ban production of these materials for use in nuclear weapons.

Lead international efforts to shut down nuclear programs in North Korea, Iran, and elsewhere.
We must show determined leadership to end the nuclear weapons program in North Korea and prevent the development of nuclear weapons in places such as Iran. North Korea has sold ballistic missiles and technology in the past. The North Koreans have made it clear to the world—and to the terrorists—that they are open for business and will sell to the highest bidder. But while this administration has been fixated on Iraq, the nuclear

dangers from North Korea have multiplied. North Korea has reportedly made enough new material to make six to nine nuclear bombs. At the same time, just as we are scouring Iraq for signs of weapons of mass destruction, they appear to be working to build them next door in Iran. We will:

★ *Work toward negotiating a comprehensive agreement with North Korea that will completely, irreversibly, and verifiably end North Korea's nuclear weapons program,*

★ *Continue the current six-nation negotiations with North Korea, but be prepared to engage in direct U.S. bilateral negotiations with Pyongyang as part of those talks,*

★ *Join our European allies to offer Iran a simple deal—to supply Tehran with the nuclear fuel it needs for peaceful energy purposes and recapture any spent fuel so it cannot be redirected into a weapons program,*

★ *Strengthen the Nuclear Nonproliferation Treaty by offering every country a deal like the one we propose for Iran: nuclear fuel in exchange for an agreement to shut down enrichment and reprocessing facilities.*

Enhance international efforts to stop trafficking in nuclear materials.

We must also strengthen our ability to prevent trafficking in bomb-making materials and components. We will:

★ *Work with the international community to toughen export controls, stiffen penalties, and strengthen law*

*enforcement and intelligence sharing so that disasters
like the AQ Khan network do not ever happen again,*

★ *Work through the United Nations and international
treaties to outlaw trade in the technologies and weapons
of mass destruction,*

★ *Increase participation in the Proliferation Security
Initiative, which provides for inspection of shipments
that might hide dangerous materials.*

**Make prevention of nuclear terrorism a top national
security priority.**

We will:

★ *Appoint a Presidential Coordinator who will focus
exclusively on directing a top line effort to secure all
nuclear weapons and materials around the world and
ensure that efforts to prevent nuclear terrorism are
prioritized and integrated into a comprehensive plan,*

★ *Instruct the Secretaries of Defense, Energy, and State
to make counter-proliferation efforts a major emphasis
in every element of national security policy.*

PROMOTING DEMOCRACY, DEVELOPMENT, PEACE, AND SECURITY

Promoting democracy, human rights, and the rule of law is
vital to our long-term security—Americans are safer in a
world of democracies. We will restore America's ability and
commitment to act as a credible force for democracy and
human rights, starting in Iraq. Torture is unacceptable—we

both share the American people's revulsion at the incidents at Abu Ghraib and other detention facilities. These acts endanger the lives of our soldiers, make their mission harder to accomplish, and contradict everything that the brave men and women of our armed forces are fighting to defend. We are determined to provide the leadership needed to make sure that such behavior never occurs again. Upholding international standards for the treatment of prisoners advances America's national security, the security of our troops, and the values of our people.

Winning the peace in Iraq.

More than a year ago, President Bush stood on an aircraft carrier under a banner that proclaimed "mission accomplished." But today we know that the mission is not accomplished, hostilities have not ended, and our men and women in uniform stand almost alone.

We both voted to give the president the authority to use force as a last resort to disarm Saddam. We know that people disagree about whether America should have gone to war in Iraq. But this much is certain—the administration badly exaggerated its case, badly mishandled the responsibility to secure international support, and badly mismanaged the planning for peace. They clearly misrepresented the connection between Saddam's government and al Qaeda—and stubbornly cling to their story despite all evidence to the contrary. They did not build a true international coalition. They disdained the United Nations weapons inspection process and rushed to war without exhausting diplomatic alternatives. They did not send sufficient forces into Iraq to accomplish the mission—ignoring the advice of military leaders. And they simply had no plan to win the peace.

We must change course. The administration has begun to, in fits and starts, by taking up suggestions that many Democrats, including both of us, first made more than a year ago. But they continue to drag their heels, and that is unacceptable.

Our troops in Iraq have not had the clarity of mission, the equipment, and the international support they need and deserve. Our helicopter pilots have flown battlefield missions without the best available anti-missile systems. Too many of our nation's finest troops have died in attacks because thousands were deployed to Iraq without the best bulletproof vests, and there is a shortage of armored vehicles on the ground. Thousands of National Guardsmen and reservists have been forced to leave their families and jobs for more than a year—with no end in sight—because this administration ignored the pressing need for a true coalition. When we are in the White House, that will all change.

Having gone to war, we cannot afford to fail at peace. We must take immediate measures to prevent Iraq from becoming a failed state that inevitably would become a haven for terrorists and a destabilizing force in the Middle East.

We must now forge a new policy based on what we know and on what will be most effective. We still have an opportunity to prevent Iraq from becoming a failed state and a haven for global terrorists and Islamic extremists. We can still succeed in promoting stability, democracy, protection of minority and women's rights, and peace in the region if we construct and follow a realistic path.

To accomplish this, America must do the hard work to get the world's major political powers to join in this mission. We must build a real coalition of countries to work together to achieve our mission in Iraq; the international community shares the stakes—they should share the political and military burdens. To do that, of course, we must share responsibility with those nations that answer our call, and treat them with respect. We must lead—and we must listen. We should:

★ *Make the creation of a stable and secure environment our immediate priority in Iraq in order to lay the foundation for a sustainable democracy,*

★ *Fully internationalize the non-Iraqi security and reconstruction personnel in Iraq, to share the costs and burdens, end the continuing perception of a U.S. occupation, and help coordinate reconstruction efforts, draft the constitution, and organize elections,*

★ *Persuade NATO to deploy a significant portion of the force that will be needed to secure and win the peace in Iraq,*

★ *Plan for Iraq's future by working with our allies to forgive Iraq's multi-billion dollar debt and by supporting the development of a new Iraqi constitution and the political arrangements needed to protect minority rights. We will also convene a regional conference with Iraq's*

*neighbors to secure a pledge to respect Iraq's borders
and not to interfere in its internal affairs,*

★ *Launch a massive and accelerated training effort to build
Iraqi security forces that can provide real security for the
Iraqi people, including a major role for NATO.*

Middle East peace.

We are fundamentally committed to the security of our
ally Israel and the creation of a comprehensive, just and
lasting peace between Israel and its neighbors. Our special relationship with Israel is based on the unshakable
foundation of shared values and mutual commitment to
democracy, and we will ensure that under all circumstances Israel retains the qualitative edge for its national
security and its right to self-defense. We believe that
Jerusalem is the capital of Israel and should remain an
undivided city accessible to people of all faiths. We will:

★ *Bring genuine resolve and direct personal involvement to
ending the Israeli-Palestinian conflict,*

★ *Work to transform the Palestinian Authority to promote
new and responsible leadership, committed to fighting
terror and promoting democracy,*

★ *Support the creation of a democratic Palestinian state
dedicated to living in peace and security side by side
with the Jewish State of Israel. We believe that the creation of a Palestinian state should resolve the issue of
Palestinian refugees by allowing them to settle there,
rather than in Israel,*

★ *Understand that it is unrealistic to expect that the outcome of final status negotiations will be a full and complete return to the armistice lines of 1949—and we understand that all final status negotiations must be mutually agreed on,*

★ *Work to end direct and indirect financing of Palestinian terrorist organizations and anti-Israeli propaganda in the news media and schools.*

Africa.

U.S. engagement in Africa should reflect its vital significance to U.S. interests as well as the moral imperative to help a continent struggling with the scourge of disease and persistent poverty. The HIV/AIDS pandemic in southern and eastern Africa is a massive human tragedy. It is also a security risk of the highest order that threatens to plunge nations into chaos. Chronic and debilitating hunger also threatens the very survival of communities where investment in agriculture has suffered for over a decade. We are committed to bringing the full weight of American leadership to bear against these challenges.

We must also work with the United Nations and Africa's regional organizations to address Africa's persistent, disproportionate share of the world's weak, failing states and chronic armed conflicts, and promote sustainable economic development. We support extension of the African Growth and Opportunity Act, which provides a door to a brighter future for many of the continent's poorest countries. We will also support effective relief efforts when there is a humanitarian crisis—particularly at this moment in Darfur, Sudan, where genocide is underway. And we will continue to promote policies to support democracy, economic reform, and respect for human rights.

Asia.

We believe that we must engage with China effectively to secure Chinese adherence to international trade, non-proliferation, and human rights standards. We are committed to a "One China" policy and will continue to support a peaceful resolution of cross-Straits issues. We support Taiwan's vibrant democracy and robust economy and will maintain America's commitment to provide Taiwan with defensive weapons. We must strengthen the already strong relationship with Japan. We will actively seek to enhance relations with our historic ally South Korea in order to advance our collaborative efforts on economic and security issues. We will continue to work together with these countries to bring about the complete, irreversible and verifiable end to North Korea's nuclear weapons program. We must also work with our friends, India and Pakistan, in their efforts to resolve longstanding differences.

Europe.

We are committed to restoring our alliances with European countries and revitalizing the Atlantic partnership that has been badly damaged by the Bush administration. Throughout the 20th century, America's most trusted and reliable allies were the democracies of Europe; together, the two sides of the Atlantic ensured that democracy and free markets prevailed against all challenges. The Bush administration has allowed the Atlantic partnership to erode, leaving the United States dangerously isolated from its indispensable allies. We look forward to working together with a prosperous and unified Europe in meeting today's security challenges and expanding the global economy. We also understand that alliances involve mutual obligations; we will expect our European allies to share the responsibility of meeting our mutual security needs. And we will ensure that NATO remains strong, continuing to consolidate peace in Europe even as the alliance takes on new tasks in Afghanistan and Iraq.

We are committed to the resumption of genuinely active, high-level participation in the Northern Ireland peace process. By pro-actively supporting the leaders in Northern Ireland and the Irish and British Governments, we will work to help achieve the full implementation of the Good Friday Agreement, including the restoration of the Assembly, the assurance of the permanence of the democratic institutions, the demilitarization of Northern Ireland, an end to all paramilitarism, progress on equality and human rights, and a police service that fairly represents and is widely supported by the people of Northern Ireland. We support giving undocumented workers who have lived and worked here for five years, who pay taxes, and who are successfully screened for security purposes, a path to citizenship. We are also aware of the deportee cases and will take a fresh look at them.

Latin America and the Caribbean.

We believe that it is time to create a new Community of the Americas that reflects our close relationship with our regional neighbors. We will return U.S.-Latin American relations to a place marked by dialogue, consensus, and concerted action to address common concerns. We understand that our collective security and prosperity are furthered by mutual efforts to promote democracy, generate wealth, reduce income disparities, and provide sound environmental stewardship. We are committed to strong and steady support for democratic processes and institutions in our hemisphere, and believe that we should exercise our considerable diplomatic and moral force in support of democratically elected leaders. We will make relations with Mexico a priority in order to best address economic, environmental, and social issues of concern.

We will increase efforts to combat drug-trafficking throughout the Caribbean and assist in combating corruption so that funds made available for development are used appropriately. We will support economic development to increase employment and economic opportunity, reducing incentives for emigration by dangerous and life-threatening means.

We support effective and peaceful strategies to end the Castro regime as soon as possible and enable the Cuban people to take their rightful place in the democratic Community of the Americas. We will work with the international community to increase political and diplomatic pressure on the Castro regime to release all political prisoners, support civil society, promote the important work of Cuban dissidents, and begin a process of genuine political reform. We support a policy of principled travel to Cuba that promotes family unity and people-to-people contacts through educational and cultural exchanges.

Global health.

We believe that addressing global health challenges is a humanitarian obligation and a national security imperative. Epidemics can decimate societies and contribute to failed states, which can become bases for terrorists and other criminal elements. We will restore American leadership to the international community's effort to combat the HIV/AIDS pandemic. We will double U.S. funding to fight AIDS, tuberculosis, and malaria to $30 billion by 2008. And we will ensure that U.S. contributions to the Global Fund to Fight AIDS, Tuberculosis, and Malaria are substantially increased above the Bush administration's current funding levels. We are committed to maximizing the effectiveness of our funds by providing those who need treatment with safe, effective, and affordable generic drugs.

A strong global public health system is essential to effectively combating bio-terror threats. Our global health policy will bring the best of our scientific knowledge, financial resources, management skills, and compassion to the challenge of improving health conditions around the world. And we will restore America's leadership in global health by rejecting policies driven by ideology instead of science.

Together, we can make our country a safer America, a stronger America, a respected America. We can do it in a way that safeguards all the greatness of America, by protecting our people, securing our homeland, and reinforcing our values—faith and family, duty and service, individual freedom and a common purpose to build one nation under God. We can do it in a way that keeps faith with the best measures of American leadership around the world—the builder of alliances, the defender of freedom, the champion of human rights. We can do it, and we will.

HOMELAND SECURITY

The first responsibility of government is to protect its citizens from harm. We have made some progress since the terrible attacks of September 11th, but we have not done nearly enough. Today the Bush administration has no coherent plan for domestic defense. Our intelligence services remain fragmented and lack coordination. Millions of shipping containers arrive at American ports every year without being searched. Our borders are not secure. Our chemical plants are vulnerable to attack. Across America, police officers, firefighters, and other first responders still lack the information, protective gear, and communications equipment needed to do their jobs safely and successfully.

We offer a new strategy for homeland security that addresses five major challenges. Our plan will:

★ *Improve our ability to gather, analyze, and share information so we can track terrorists down and stop them before they cause harm,*

★ *Better secure our airports, seaports, and borders,*

★ *Harden likely terrorist targets and critical infrastructure,*

★ *Improve domestic readiness,*

★ *Protect freedom and justice even as we protect our people and our homeland.*

Better intelligence.

The war on terror begins with good intelligence. Shockingly, many of the same flaws in intelligence-sharing that allowed terrorists to slip in and out of America before September 11th still exist. The government has missed its own deadlines for upgrading and integrating security databases and still fails to share information with the state and local law enforcement agencies on the frontlines. This must change. We will:

★ *Create a true Director of National Intelligence with real control over all intelligence personnel and budgets,*

★ *Transform our intelligence services to ensure that they have sufficient personnel with the skills, languages, training and orientation needed to meet today's threats,*

★ *Break down the bureaucratic barriers that prevent vital information-sharing between intelligence agencies and law enforcement at both the national and local levels, including granting security clearances to state and local officials where appropriate.*

More secure borders.

Our borders are far too porous, especially to cargo that comes by sea or air. Our plan will improve security at our borders, seaports, and airports. We will:

★ *Improve the detection equipment in our shipping systems,*

★ *Ensure that private companies obtain adequate information about items they are shipping,*

★ *Work with other nations to increase inspections of seaborne cargo,*

★ *Adopt tighter controls on air cargo, tons of which goes uninspected every day,*

★ *Replace the unsuccessful airport screening system with a new system that identifies security threats while honoring American values,*

★ *Work with Canada, Mexico, and Caribbean nations to strengthen border controls, using better technology and more personnel to improve inspections while speeding up commerce.*

Hardened targets.

We will launch a major effort to harden our critical infrastructure and most vulnerable targets—from chemical and nuclear plants to rails, tunnels and key cyber networks—and better protect them from attack. For example, there are more than 100 chemical plants where an attack could endanger more than one million people, and the

FBI has warned that al Qaeda may target our chemical industry. The Bush administration was moving toward a commonsense solution that would set minimum standards for safety at chemical plants—but after heavy lobbying by the chemical industry, they backed down. We will put safety first. We will:

★ *Better protect nuclear plants and weapons facilities as an urgent priority,*

★ *Require new security standards at chemical plants, including more guards, better fencing, and use of less dangerous chemicals where possible,*

★ *Improve railroad and subway security by taking steps such as providing chemical release detectors and tightening security at critical entry points.*

Domestic readiness.

First responders are the first ones up the stairs in the event of an emergency, and it is wrong that today they are last in line when it comes to this administration's budgets. Our plan will improve domestic readiness so people on the frontlines have the training and equipment to respond to any attack with all the speed, skill, and strength required. In the end, homeland security is not about changing the alert from yellow to orange; the colors of safety are firefighter red, EMT white, and police officer blue. We will:

★ *Provide assistance to police and fire departments to end serious shortages of manpower, training, and equipment,*

★ Modernize our emergency warning system to provide localized warnings, treat frontline fighters as partners, and give families all the information they need,

★ Enlist citizens in homeland security efforts through an expanded AmeriCorps national service program, and a "21st Century Neighborhood Watch" initiative focused on emergency response needs.

Although there has been progress in preparing for a bioterrorist attack, we still do not have strong national leadership in planning or coordination. Our hospitals are overwhelmed and our public health system cannot handle large, lethal epidemics of disease. We lack adequate supplies, drugs, and vaccines. We will:

★ Put one person in charge of overseeing all bioterrorism programs, budgets, and strategic priorities in order to establish a coordinated, national response strategy,

★ Work with state and local leaders to establish the benchmarks for state and local preparedness required by law and still missing today,

★ Revitalize our public health system to improve monitoring of disease outbreaks,

★ Harness America's bioscience genius to improve preparedness for a bioterror attack by creating a Medical Arsenal of Democracy dedicated to speeding drug and vaccine development,

★ *Strengthen our hospitals and ensure they have emergency plans to address a surge in medical needs under mass casualty and exposure conditions.*

Guarding liberty.

We must always remember that terrorists do not just target our lives; they target our way of life. And so we must be on constant guard not to sacrifice the freedom we are fighting to protect. We will strengthen some parts of the Patriot Act, like the restrictions on money laundering, and improve other aspects of it, like information sharing. At the same time, we will revise parts of the Patriot Act such as the library provisions to better protect our freedom. We will ensure government can take all needed steps to fight terror. Our government should never round up innocent people only because of their religion or ethnicity, and should always honor our Constitution. We believe in an America where freedom is what we fight for—not what we give up.

★

An Energy Independent America

No strategy for American security is complete without a plan to end America's dangerous dependence on Mideast oil. We consume 2.5 million barrels of oil per day from the Middle East. Our economy depends on oil controlled by some of the world's most repressive regimes. This is a real threat to our national security, our economy, and our environment.

Dependence on foreign oil is a *security* problem because it forces us to rely on volatile regions ruled by some of the world's most authoritarian regimes. We believe a strong America must no longer rely on the cooperation of regimes that may not share our values, and we are not willing to risk a future in which our young men and women might have to risk their lives to protect Mideast oil supplies. We must ensure that our dependence on Mideast oil no longer hampers our ability to act as a strong moral force in the world.

★

HOW MISMANAGING THE WAR ON TERROR
HAS HURT CONSUMERS

Americans have experienced some of the highest gas prices in over three decades. These record high prices are not just the result of the Bush administration's failure to create an energy policy that moves America away from dependence on foreign oil. It is also a result of what experts call a "terror premium."

Before the war in Iraq started, oil was trading at nearly $35 per barrel and the futures market predicted that the price would drop to about $25 per barrel by June 2004. Instead, the price of oil in June rose to over $40 a barrel. Most of this $15 per barrel difference—more than 50 percent higher than expected—is attributed to security threats, unstable conditions in the Middle East and general fears of terrorism. That is the terror premium.

Experts throughout the oil and gas sector have commented on these unpredictably high prices. Daniel Yergin, a leading energy expert, has argued that anxiety and geopolitical risks have been inflating prices. Wells Fargo's chief economist argued that fear was driving up prices, noting that speculators in the oil market were betting that geopolitical turbulence would keep prices rising. Almost weekly sabotage events in both Iraq and Saudi Arabia have lent credence to this argument and continued to destabilize the oil markets. If the Bush administration had more effectively managed Iraq after the initial combat, it is reasonable to assume that the price of oil would be more stable today.

★

Dependence on foreign oil is an *economic* problem because it gives other countries that do not always share all of our key interests the power to disrupt economic growth in the United States, Europe, and East Asia by manipulating oil prices and supplies. The price of oil produced everywhere, even in the U.S., is effectively controlled by the OPEC cartel, which is dominated by Middle East producers. OPEC's stronghold on global oil prices exposes us to price spikes and supply interruptions over which we have little or no control. Rising oil prices over the last several years have already placed a large burden on U.S. citizens and businesses. Together with record increases in the cost of health care, college tuition, and a drop in income, rising gas prices are a burdensome part of the middle-class squeeze that is making it harder and harder for millions of families to make ends meet. We should never forget the lesson of the 1970s, when OPEC producers used the "oil weapon" to cause a price spike that hamstrung our economy for years, slowed growth, accelerated inflation, and caused one of the worst recessions since the Great Depression.

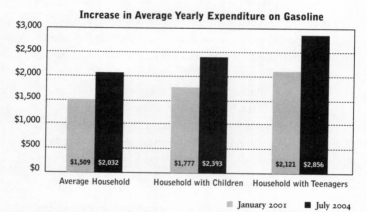

Increase in Average Yearly Expenditure on Gasoline

Average Household: $1,509 / $2,032
Household with Children: $1,777 / $2,393
Household with Teenagers: $2,121 / $2,856

■ January 2001　■ July 2004

[Department of Energy, Household Vehicles Energy Consumption 1994, Table 5.2, August 1997; AAA, Fuel Gauge Report, 7/13/04]

And dependence on oil is an *environmental and health* problem. The oil products we use to power our cars and trucks causes smog and other forms of air pollution, and contributes to the growing risk of climate change—a risk that, despite the Bush administration's refusal to acknowledge it, is widely recognized throughout the scientific community.

For decades, we have been stuck on an energy crisis roller coaster. Gas prices rise and people talk about the need for a new energy policy. When gas prices drop, people drop the issue. If unrest erupts in the Middle East, people talk about the need to address our energy needs. When prices drop and stability returns, we turn to another topic. It is time to get off this ride and chart a new course.

We believe a strong America must move toward energy independence. In the short-term, we can lower energy costs and help working families. We can provide relief to our farmers who will spend an additional $1.3 billion on gas this year, our truck drivers who will spend an additional $5 billion, and our airlines that will spend an additional $4.5 billion on jet fuel. And for the long-term, we have a comprehensive energy plan to make America independent of Mideast oil.

And not only can we can achieve it, we can make America stronger, and produce great benefits for our people along the way. Achieving energy independence will improve our ability to protect our values and interests around the world. It will reduce energy costs for our families. It will create high-paying new jobs. And it will improve our environment and make our people healthier.

This administration has done nothing as gas prices have soared to record levels. Even the administration's own economists have found that their energy plan will do nothing to reduce gas prices. This president's approach to energy policy leaves America shackled to foreign oil—dependent and vulnerable. There are few challenges facing America today that affect our future in so many ways as the challenge of achieving independence from Mideast oil. Yet it is a challenge that the current administration has completely failed to address.

The principle of the Bush administration's energy plan is more, not less, dependence on oil. Although the president has embraced the far-off solution of hydrogen fuel cells for tomorrow's transportation system, he lacks a balanced plan for energy diversification today. The centerpiece of the administration's energy plan is to open up the environmentally sensitive Arctic National Wildlife Refuge for drilling—a proposal that promises only minimal improvement in our domestic oil supplies but will inflict permanent damage on the Refuge's lands and wildlife.

The Bush administration contends that a strategy for energy independence is not viable because it relies too heavily on government intervention in energy markets.

Our current policies cost taxpayers billions of dollars today, and create even greater costs for both government and business tomorrow. We need to invest more wisely and lead the country toward energy independence rather than give handouts to special interests that perpetuate our reliance on oil.

We have a comprehensive plan to lead America to energy independence. Our plan will unleash the full force of American optimism and ingenuity—the genius of our scientists and engineers and the century-long adaptability of our automakers. We invented and built the cars, home energy systems, and power plants of today. And we can invent and build the energy-efficient products and technologies of tomorrow.

Sixty-two years ago, Franklin Roosevelt brought together America's best minds and most innovative technologies in a crash project to develop nuclear weapons before they could be developed and deployed by our enemies. The Manhattan Project conveyed a sense of national urgency and focus with an unprecedented partnership between public resources and private innovation. Later, America launched another bold initiative known as the Apollo Project to accelerate our search to explore the new frontier of space. Changing the way we produce and use energy is no less urgent a national priority. Our energy plan will marshal the same concentration of brainpower, willpower, and innovation to create new energy sources and technologies and put us on a path toward energy independence. We will pursue three avenues at once by:

★   *Exploring and developing new energy sources,*

★   *Improving energy efficiency and developing renewable energy technologies,*

★   *Diversifying existing energy sources and reducing prices.*

This plan will generate 500,000 new jobs within a decade, and position America at the leading edge of some of the world's most profitable industries.

Exploring and developing new energy sources.

Our energy plan will embrace a simple but revolutionary goal: harnessing new energy sources to power the world we live in. We believe sources like the sun, wind, and a rich array of crops can provide us with secure forms of energy at reasonable costs for the rest of this century—but only if we start exploring and developing them today. Our plan sets the goal of producing 20 percent of our electricity from renewable sources by the year 2020, reducing our reliance on oil, improving our environment, and creating new "cash crops."

To reach that goal, our plan will:

★ *Expand the Production Tax Credit for wind and biomass energy to cover the full array of renewable energy sources,*

★ *Increase Department of Energy research into renewable energy sources and their applications,*

★ *Create a new public-private partnership to help finance renewable energy research and development in the private sector,*

★ *Our plan will also expand the use of renewable fuels to power our cars, trucks, and SUVs. We will put 100,000 hydrogen-fueled vehicles on the road by 2010, and 2.5 million by 2020.*

To meet these goals we will:

★ *Increase the use of renewable fuels such as ethanol to 5 billion gallons by 2012,*

★ *Expand federally sponsored research into renewable fuels for automobiles,*

★ *Create a Hydrogen Institute to unite scientists and researchers in the drive to accelerate hydrogen fuel cell and other advanced fuel technology.*

★

FUELING RURAL ECONOMIES

Investing in energy independence and renewable energy sources is critical to the growth of the rural economy and the security of our nation's energy supply. Renewable fuels like ethanol and biodiesel decrease our dependence on foreign oil. Instead of sending billions of dollars to unstable and often hostile regimes, we would divert that money back to farmers and Main Streets here at home.

We must ensure that at least 5 billion gallons of renewable fuel is part of America's energy supply by 2012. This standard provides a much-needed boost to rural areas by creating new jobs and adding value to products farmers produce. For example, the use of corn and other commodities for ethanol production adds 20 to 40 cents to every bushel of corn. Not only do farmers benefit from the higher price, an increasing number of farmers are joining together in cooperatives to build ethanol production facilities—thereby directly taking advantage of the value-added market through ownership.

In addition to increasing the use of biofuels, the renewable fuels standards would provide a shot in the arm to our still struggling national economy. According to the Renewable Fuels Association, by 2012, the standard would add $156 billion to the Gross Domestic Product (GDP), spur $5.3 billion new capital investments, and create 214,000 new jobs. In rural America, the RFS would mean an increase of $1.3 billion in annual farm income.

Opportunities in rural America do not end with renewable fuels. In many states, individual farmers and ranchers lease their property to wind power companies and receive an annual payment for having wind turbines on their property. With the right leadership, this could become a "cash crop" for many other farmers and ranchers around the country and stabilize rural economies as well as meet the growing demand for clean sources of electricity.

★

New renewable and affordable energy sources are not a science fiction dream. With more aggressive leadership and a real plan, we can expand their use today and build an energy-efficient America tomorrow.

★

BENEFITS OF THE RENEWABLE PORTFOLIO STANDARD

Renewable energy can help solve multiple problems: rising energy prices, energy supply shortages and disruptions, and harmful air pollution. A national renewable portfolio standard (RPS) to provide 20 percent of U.S. electricity from sources like wind, solar, and biomass energy by 2020 would have essentially no cost for consumers, according to a recent study by the U.S. Department of Energy. Because they are home-grown, renewable energy sources can also increase energy security and create local jobs.

Diversifying the power supply by developing America's renewable energy resources creates a more competitive market, which can reduce natural gas prices and save consumers and businesses money on their energy bills. In addition, renewable energy is not subject to the price volatility that plagues natural gas power plants.

The RPS will stimulate investment in new renewable energy throughout the nation, creating jobs and lifting incomes in rural areas as well as in the high tech and manufacturing sectors. With a strong domestic renewable energy industry, the U.S. economy will benefit from this industry's large export potential.

Adopting a strong national renewable portfolio standard will also help to improve the environment, reducing U.S. carbon dioxide emissions as well as emissions of nitrogen oxides, sulfur dioxide, and mercury, will help address acid rain, smog, water contamination, and will limit our contribution to global warming.

★

Improving energy efficiency and reliability.

The energy economy of the future depends on the development of cleaner, more efficient technology and production methods to make better use of existing energy sources. We can make immediate progress on energy efficiency simply by making a national commitment to do so, with our government leading by example. With respect to energy efficiency in our office buildings, homes, and communities, our plan will:

★ *Cut the federal government's energy bills by 20 percent by 2020, saving an estimated $14 billion for taxpayers,*

★ *Challenge and help state and local governments, corporations, universities, hospitals, and small businesses to meet the same 20 percent energy efficiency goal,*

★ *Provide tax incentives for "smart building" practices to spur energy-efficient construction and renovation methods.*

Nearly 70 percent of the oil Americans consume is burned in cars, trucks, trains, and planes. Energy-efficiency in transportation can be rapidly improved, just as it was during the energy crisis of the 1970s, without sacrificing consumer choice. At the same time, we can enhance U.S. automakers' competitive advantage in the global automotive marketplace of the future. Our plan will:

★ *Update and strengthen our fuel-efficiency standards,*

★ *Create new tax incentives for automakers to build the new, more efficient automobiles of the future,*

★ *Provide tax incentives for families to purchase more energy-efficient cars, trucks, and SUVs.*

We will work to create better, more efficient technologies for producing electricity, and ensure that our people have access to a secure and reliable supply of electricity at all times. Our plan includes:

★ *Mandatory, enforceable reliability standards for our electric grid that will help avoid blackouts,*

★ *Public-private partnerships to make our power systems more flexible, resilient, and self-healing—and more environmentally friendly than ever before.*

We believe that coal should be part of the solution to our energy and environmental challenges. We need to harness technology to develop clean electric power from coal. At the same time, we believe that we need clear benchmarks and a flexible framework to measure the emissions performance of existing and new uses of coal. Our "clean coal" plan will:

★ *Invest $10 billion over the next decade to transform the current generation of coal-fired utility plants into cleaner and more energy-efficient plants,*

★ *Develop new technologies to generate clean electric power from coal,*

★ *Employ flexible, market-based strategies to reduce utility plant emissions of nitrogen oxide, sulfur dioxide, mercury, and carbon dioxide while rewarding companies that develop new and cleaner technologies.*

Expanding new energy sources while improving the efficiency of existing sources will go a long way toward reducing dependence on Mideast oil. At the same time, it will dramatically reduce the environmental and health damage being created by our current energy use. Even if we only partly accomplish our goals, we will reverse current trends toward greater dependence on oil, more pollution, and higher costs for businesses and consumers.

Diversifying and reducing prices for current energy sources.

Even in the limited universe of fossil fuel sources, we can do more to expand supplies and lower costs right now— without damaging the environment. We must take immediate steps to reduce gasoline prices. Our plan will:

★ *Temporarily suspend the Bush administration's practice of "topping off" the Strategic Petroleum Reserve until prices decrease,*

★ *Aggressively "jawbone" oil producing nations to
   keep production levels high enough to stabilize oil
   and gasoline prices.*

We should explore opportunities to replace OPEC producers with non-OPEC sources of oil. Although this step
cannot be the centerpiece for a 21st century energy strategy,
we can explore domestic and non-OPEC sources for oil
without new damage to the environment. We will:

★ *Develop domestic supplies in areas already open for
   exploration, including the western and central Gulf of
   Mexico and Alaska's National Petroleum Reserve,*

★ *Work to increase the availability of oil from countries
   outside the OPEC cartel, including Russia, Canada, and
   certain areas of Africa.*

Finally, we will make a major push to expand the availability—and hold down the price—of the cleanest form
of fossil fuel: natural gas. While we may never get back
to the days of unlimited natural gas supplies at very low
prices, we can make immediate progress to improve supplies and prices. Our plan will:

★ *Pursue a North American Energy Initiative, a long-term
   partnership with Canada and Mexico to develop and
   expand our continent's abundant natural gas reserves,*

★ *Speed construction of an Alaska Natural Gas Pipeline
   to help move the 35 trillion cubic feet of known natural
   gas reserves on the North Slope of Alaska into the
   U.S. marketplace,*

★ *Ensure a fair and well-functioning natural gas market to prevent abuses and supply shortages like those that recently threatened blackouts and huge price spikes in the western United States.*

Overall, our plan will tackle dependence on Mideast oil, and address the associated risks to our national security, our economy, our environment, and our health and quality of life. It will do this by expanding new and old energy sources, deploying new technologies, increasing efficiency, and producing cleaner energy.

Given that sixty-five percent of the world's oil reserves are in the Middle East, America will never be able to drill our way to energy independence. But if we have the will and the imagination to declare our commitment to energy independence today, we can achieve it tomorrow. We can create jobs and build a stronger country. We can once again make America the energy and transportation capital of the world, and make America the world's best steward of the environment we all share.

CHAPTER TWO

★

OPPORTUNITY

I believe the measure of

a strong economy

is a growing middle class,

where every American

has the opportunity to succeed.

John Edwards

★

Building a Strong Economy

A strong America begins at home. We must restore the broad economic growth that expands and strengthens the middle class and leaves a stronger foundation to build prosperity for all our people in the generations to come.

The great promise of America is simple: a better life for all who work for it. It was a revolutionary idea 228 years ago, and it is still remarkable today—no society on earth before ours made such a promise to its people, and it is up to each generation of Americans to keep it alive, and pass it on.

The heart of that promise has always been the middle class, the greatest engine of economic strength the world has ever known. When the middle class grows in size and security, our economy grows stronger.

We share faith in American economic growth and the American dream: that we can strengthen our middle class and make it bigger, that we can offer a better future to all those who work hard and act responsibly.

Opportunity for all, special privileges for none. Simple, straightforward guideposts for equality that have been the watchwords of the Democratic Party. That's what we believe in.

But this White House values wealth over hard work, gives special treatment to the most fortunate at everyone else's expense, and defends the tax breaks companies use to send jobs overseas.

Today, our nation faces immense economic challenges: spiraling health care costs, historic job loss, rising tuition and energy costs, and a looming Social Security and Medicare solvency challenge. The Bush administration has ignored each of these challenges, focusing all their effort instead on the defense of massive tax cuts for the most fortunate that have driven America deeply into debt. These kinds of policies did not create long-term growth in the 1980s, and they are not working now.

In the 1990s, we had a strategy of fiscal discipline that rewarded work and invested in the potential of our people. That strategy helped lay a foundation for the economic growth that lifted up all Americans. Not only were nearly 23 million jobs created but family income went up for all income groups, while poverty and unemployment fell to the lowest levels in decades and our nation went from large deficits to record surpluses.

The American dream means ensuring economic growth that lifts the incomes, the opportunities, and the hopes of all Americans. President Bush is asking America to lower its sights and its standards. He is telling us that even though he is on track to be the first president since Herbert Hoover to preside over net job loss; even though wages have gone down while health, energy, child care and tuition costs have shot up—this is the best America's economy can do. We do not accept such a pessimistic view of America's economic potential. We believe America can do better.

It is time for a new direction. It is time for a stronger America. It is time to be the America we are meant to be.

So when it comes to the economy, our pledge to America is not new at all—it is the age-old promise of America; we are just going to keep it.

In our administration, every day, we will work to make sure that no matter who you are, where you come from, or what your background is, as an American you will live in a nation that offers all the possibility your hard work and God-given talent can bring. You will live in a nation with responsible immigration laws that strengthen our borders and recognize the human rights of the millions of families who work in our fields, our manufacturing plants, our service industry; who send their children to our schools, pay taxes, and love and embrace the America that is our home.

We have a comprehensive economic plan to keep the American promise and breathe new life into every sector of our economy. Our economic strategy recognizes that government does not create jobs or produce economic growth. Free markets, honest competition, America's entrepreneurial sprit and hard work do that. But the right public policies can foster an environment that makes strong growth and job creation easier, and the wrong policies can hurt. We understand that the right policies can promote an economic climate that will lay the foundation for private sector investment, foster vigorous competition, and strengthen the foundations of an innovative economy.

We offer America a new economic plan that will put jobs first. We believe in progress that brings prosperity for all Americans, not just for those who are already successful. We believe that good jobs will help strengthen and expand the middle class, the strongest middle class the world has ever known.

We believe Americans are the smartest, toughest competitors in the world. And we believe companies can keep jobs in America without sacrificing competitiveness.

CREATING GOOD JOBS

The opportunity to build a better future starts with a good job. It has always been that way. From the time when most people worked the land, through the Industrial Revolution and into the Information Age, the opportunity for work, the rewards from work, and the dignity of work have made Americans successful and America strong.

In February 2002, the Bush administration said America, under their leadership, would create nearly 6 million jobs by mid-2004. Instead, to date, the economy has lost more than 1 million private-sector jobs under President Bush. We are 7 million jobs short of the administration's own prediction—and that does not even take into consideration the millions of Americans who have given up looking for work or who are working part-time because they cannot find the full-time work they need to support their families. Over 75 percent of the new jobs being created today are being created in low-wage industries and are 13 percent less likely to offer health care benefits. Indeed the new jobs that are finally being created pay an average of $9,000 less, making it even harder for the middle class to get ahead.

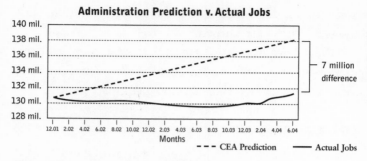

[Council of Economic Advisors, "Economic Report of the President, 2002," Bureau of Labor Statistics]

And job losses are not the only problem on the employment front—the jobs that are being created generally pay less, offer fewer benefits, and are of lower quality than the jobs we are losing. In fact, jobs in industries that are expanding pay an average of $9,160 a year less than jobs in industries that are shrinking. More than three quarters of all the jobs created over the last year pay less than average wages.

Our plan will reverse the job losses of the Bush-Cheney years and lay a foundation that will help our economy create 10 million new jobs over the first four years. Our plan is based on the proven economic policies of the 1990s—policies that created nearly 23 million jobs over eight years. And our plan is designed to create high-paying, high-quality jobs.

Our economic strategy begins with an all-out effort to jump start the growth of high-paying jobs. It will reduce taxes for businesses that create jobs here in the United States, while eliminating tax incentives to move jobs overseas. It calls for investing in our manufacturing scientific and technological future, by restoring fiscal discipline. It calls for reducing the costs of job creation by tackling rising health care and energy costs. And it will ensure that we have the best educated and most highly skilled workers. Our plan will fight to protect the jobs of today and create the high-wage jobs of tomorrow.

First, we will immediately move to change our tax laws and put an end to rules that actually encourage companies to send American jobs overseas. Instead, we will offer tax cuts to companies that create jobs here at home. Our plan will:

★ *Close the foreign tax deferral loophole that encourages companies to send jobs overseas,*

★ *Cut tax rates for 99 percent of taxpaying U.S. businesses by using the savings from ending deferral and offshore tax havens to cut corporate tax rates by five percent,*

★ *Jump start job creation with a New Jobs Tax Credit that will give manufacturers, other business affected by outsourcing, and small businesses a break on federal payroll taxes for every new job created in America,*

★ *Eliminate capital gains for start-up investments in small businesses.*

Because our manufacturing sector is the critical backbone of our economy and has been hit hardest by job losses, we will make a special effort to create new manufacturing jobs and help smaller manufacturers survive and thrive in the global economy. In addition to lowering taxes for manufacturers who create jobs on our shores, our plan will:

★ *Catalyze the creation of new private investment corporations to give small and medium-sized manufacturers access to the capital they need to expand operations and create new jobs,*

★ *Invest in initiatives to create high-technology manufacturing "clusters" around research institutions,*

★ *Help small manufacturers innovate and grow through the Manufacturing Extension Partnership and Advanced Technology Program, which the Bush administration has sought to shut down.*

★

AMERICAN INVESTMENTS IN RESEARCH AND NEW COMPANIES CREATE JOBS, LAUNCH INDUSTRIES, AND IMPROVE OUR LIVES

Government funding for research and development has helped launch some of the most important and successful businesses in America. Startup capital and early stage loans can turn one entrepreneur's big idea into a Fortune 500 company.

Apple Computers grew out of Steve Jobs' parents' garage with the help of a venture capital loan provided by the Small Business Investment Corporation. SBIC helped FedEx become the first company in history to earn $1 billion within a decade of its launch, hiring tens of thousands of people along the way.

The Advanced Technology Program funded research that helped develop digital mammography—a major breakthrough in accuracy, efficiency, and access to a critical test that has helped millions of women and saved lives. An ATP investment in powerful micro-technologies that make it faster and easier to conduct DNA analysis is helping us understand human genetics, open new avenues in the fight to cure and manage diseases like cancer and AIDS, and to cut health care costs.

The Manufacturing Extension Partnership (MEP) has helped save thousands of jobs by providing expert advice to small manufacturers across the country. The MEP introduces manufacturers to proven strategies that improve efficiency, cut costs, increase profitability, and save jobs as a result.

★

We will draw on our experience with small businesses to create tax incentives that encourage investment in small businesses. We will help small businesses pay for health care and create jobs. And we will promote a Small Business Opportunity Fund to expand microlending.

★

KILVERT AND FORBES:
JOHN KERRY'S SMALL BUSINESS

"After dinner in Boston one evening in 1979, a friend and I were looking for cookies in Faneuil Hall. Fortunately for us, we could not find any. When all we found was some empty retail space, an idea was born: Kilvert and Forbes, a cookie and muffin shop that we opened later that year.

"It was a late-night inspiration. I had always had an entrepreneurial spirit in me, and this great business opportunity allowed me to put it to use. My favorites were our brownies, but I cannot tell you how hard it was to get the ingredients just right.

"Fulfilling my American Dream of owning a business was a challenge and I learned a lot about what it means to be part of the American economy. I had to hire a staff and deal with payroll and taxes. I had to get permits, inspections, do the purchasing, get deliveries, and set up orders. It taught me a lot about paperwork, hassles, the bottom line, and government. So when I served as a member and later as Chairman of the Senate Small Business Committee, I knew how important it was for government to work for small business owners, not against them.

"As president, I will bring the lessons of owning and working in a small business to the Oval Office and fight for these important members of the American economy."

—John Kerry

★

If today's global economy means anything, it means this: new jobs are increasingly tied to new exports. Today, one in every five American factory jobs depends on exports—and those jobs pay more than other jobs. Open markets spur innovation, speed the growth of new industries, and make our businesses more competitive. We need more free trade—but it must be more fair trade also.

Free and fair trade means truly open markets where American companies compete on a level playing field. Unfortunately, time after time, the Bush Administration has failed to challenge other countries to live up to their commitments under international trade agreements. We will not stand for that.

Our plan will continue to ensure that America engages in the global economy. We must be honest in telling Americans that we cannot keep every job on our shores or bring back every lost industry. But we will fight at every turn to ensure that our workers and businesses are never put at an unfair disadvantage because our government is sitting on the sidelines instead of fighting for free and fair and expanded trade. We will:

★ *Complete a comprehensive review of all existing trade agreements within the first 120 days of our administration,*

★ *Aggressively pursue the remedies available through the World Trade Organization and under domestic trade laws to stop violations of those agreements and unfair trade practices,*

★ *Increase international pressure on China to end its manipulation of currency rates, which are subsidizing Chinese exports while inhibiting other countries' access to rapidly growing Chinese domestic markets,*

★ *Support international efforts to crack down on abuses of workers' rights and halt the exploitation of child labor,*

★ *Protect the intellectual property rights of U.S. businesses and inventors against commercial pirates and fight for U.S. access to key closed-off foreign market sectors, such as the Japanese auto market and Chinese high technology markets,*

★ *Build upon and strengthen the progress made by President Clinton in the Jordan agreement to include strong and enforceable internationally recognized labor and environmental standards in the core of new free trade agreements,*

★ *Expand trade adjustment assistance to help employees who lose their jobs because of global economic changes, including workers in the service sector.*

There are two additional challenges we face that have a huge impact on job creation. First, skyrocketing health care costs place a dangerous burden on American businesses. Our plan will hold costs down, expand access to affordable health care, and ease the burden on businesses. That will help release the capital businesses need to expand and create jobs. Second, we believe that America's dependence on foreign oil poses real risks to our security and economy. Our plan to lead America to energy independence is a great opportunity to create jobs and increase our security through new, high-profit, high-wage renewable energy industries.

RESTORING FISCAL RESPONSIBILITY IN WASHINGTON

Even as middle-class families struggle to live within increasingly tighter budgets, the federal government, under the complete control of the president and his party, is once again living large and piling up debt in the name of present and future taxpayers. Under President Bush, America has gone from record surpluses to record deficits.

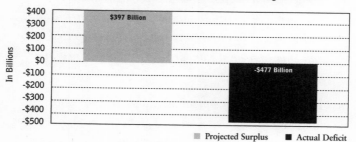

Projected Budget Surplus v. Actual Budget Deficit

Congressional Budget Office

President Bush has turned his back on the simple, bipartisan principle that guided everyone from President Clinton to Speaker Gingrich in the 1990s: pay for all proposals. Instead, the president has proposed or passed tax cuts and spending increases that would increase the deficit by more than $6 trillion over the next decade. Not once has this administration made an effort to balance new spending with new savings, or even to pay for new initiatives—including their enormous tax breaks for the wealthy.

We must restore responsibility and fiscal discipline to our government, or the debt we pass on to our children will strangle opportunity for the next generation of middle-class Americans. Massive public borrowing keeps inflation and interest rates higher than they would otherwise be, and undermines long-term investor confidence in our economy. Today's deficits also pose a serious threat to our retirement security. They are financed by borrowing from Social Security Trust Fund surpluses at a time when the retirement of the baby boom generation makes that very risky.

★

BUDGET DEFICITS HURT AMERICAN FAMILIES

Excess spending and massive tax cuts to the wealthiest Americans under President Bush have forced the government to borrow hundreds of billions of dollars. When the government borrows huge amounts of money it means there is less money available to everyone else, which increases the price of borrowing, and drives interest rates up. Families end up paying more for everything from home mortgages to student loans to car payments.

Economists have a simple rule: every one percentage point increase in the government's budget deficit forces up interest rates by almost half a percentage point. This rule is based on research by leading economists, including President Bush's current top economic adviser, N. Gregory Mankiw, and his predecessor, Glenn Hubbard.

President Bush's tax cuts—$2.3 trillion over the next decade—together with his spending proposals mean that the budget deficit will continue to increase by an average of 2.3 percent of GDP annually. According to the economists' rule of thumb, that means the Bush deficits will drive long-term interest rates up more than a full point every year.

Higher interest rates cost families money:

★ For a 30-year home mortgage of $150,000, an increase in the interest rate from 6 percent to 7 percent would raise annual payments by $1,184.

★ A one point increase adds $1,220 to the cost of a 10-year student loan.

Restoring fiscal discipline will help bring interest rates down. Federal Reserve Board Chairman Alan Greenspan credits deficit reduction for lower interest rates in the 1990s: "The lower federal deficits and, for a time, the realization of surpluses contributed significantly to improved national saving and thereby put downward pressure on real interest rates."

★

In the 1990s, fiscal responsibility created confidence in the economy, encouraged investment, and led to a record expansion. Today, we face unsustainable foreign borrowing, rising interest rates, and low consumer confidence. We will bring fiscal discipline back to Washington.

Our plan will cut the budget deficit in half within four years while reversing policies that will explode the deficit down the road if we do not act now. We will impose strict measures to promote budget discipline, including some of the same steps that helped balance the budget during the 1990s. And we will lead a major assault on corporate welfare and pork-barrel spending.

Specifically, we will:

★ *Repeal President Bush's tax cuts benefiting those earning over $200,000 a year while expanding middle-class tax cuts,*

★ *Bring back "pay-as-you-go" budget rules that require Congress to come up with offsets to pay for new spending or tax cut initiatives,*

★ *Bring back tough caps on domestic discretionary spending, reinforced by mandatory across-the-board cuts, if necessary, so that total discretionary spending, outside security and education, grows no faster than inflation,*

★ *Reduce the number of government contractors by 100,000,*

★ *Freeze the federal travel budget,*

★ *Reform student loan programs to eliminate guaranteed, government-provided profits for banks,*

★ *Enact the Kerry-McCain proposal for a Corporate Subsidy Commission to identify wasteful and economically inefficient corporate welfare items and force Congress to deal with them on a single, up-or-down vote,*

★ *Eliminate corporate tax loopholes, like the ones Enron used, which enable companies to avoid paying their fair share,*

★ *Create a constitutionally acceptable line-item veto power, to enable the president to kill pork-barrel projects unless Congress specifically re-enacts them.*

Our plan will decisively cut budget deficits while providing lower taxes for 98 percent of our families and 99 percent of our businesses. At the same time, our plan will enable us to make high-priority investments in our future, and put us in a better position to strengthen the long-term health of Social Security.

STANDING UP FOR THE GREAT AMERICAN MIDDLE CLASS: A PLAN TO EASE THE SQUEEZE

A good-paying job is only half of the basic economic equation that every family lives with. As everybody who has ever sat around the kitchen table paying bills knows, if there is less coming in than there is going out, sooner or later, something has to give.

The basic path to middle-class security is not complicated—work hard, pay your bills, save and invest in your children and your future. But if incomes are declining and costs are rising, it is hard to pay today's bills, let alone save for tomorrow.

But that is what is happening today. Today, the average American family is earning less than in 2000. At the same time, health care costs are up by nearly one-half, college tuition has increased by more than one-third, child care costs have risen by more than twice as fast as inflation, and gas and oil prices have gone through the roof. One family goes bankrupt every 19 seconds, a one-third increase since 2000.

Under President Clinton, for the first time in three decades, incomes and the standard of living rose for all Americans. But President Bush and Vice President Cheney turned away from those proven economic policies in an ideological about-face that ignored the evidence. The middle class is paying the price. Instead of working hard to get ahead, they are working hard just to get by.

It is time for a new direction. It is time to be the America we are meant to be—where the great American promise of a better life is alive and well. Our plan will lead us to an America where the middle class is expanding, our economy is thriving, and America is strong.

We will begin by restoring our values to our tax code. We want a tax code that rewards work and creates wealth for more people—not a tax code that rewards wealth and hoards it for those who already have it. Under President Bush, the tax burden has shifted onto the shoulders of those who can least afford it. With the middle class under assault like never before, we simply cannot afford President Bush's massive tax cuts for the very wealthiest. As we all know, the most fortunate Americans did well during the Clinton era—we want to reset tax rates for families making more than $200,000 to the same level they were under Bill Clinton. We will make the middle-class tax cuts permanent, as part of a fiscally responsible plan that cuts the deficit in half while investing in health care and other priorities. Under our plan,

98 percent of Americans will pay lower taxes than they would under current law.

We will provide new tax cuts to help families meet the key economic challenges of their everyday lives—health care, tuition, and child care. In total, we provide more than twice as much in new middle-class tax cuts than this administration—and every dime is fully paid for without increasing the deficit. Millions of families will receive a tax cut that will help them make ends meet without sacrificing something they should not have to give up—good health care, education, or child care. Specifically, we will offer:

★ *Tax credits to help families afford health care, including tax credits for small businesses,*

★ *A tax credit to make four years of college affordable to all Americans. Specifically, we will offer a tax credit on $4,000 of tuition for all four years of college,*

★ *A tax credit to make child care more affordable, cutting taxes by $800 for the typical middle-class family with two children in child care.*

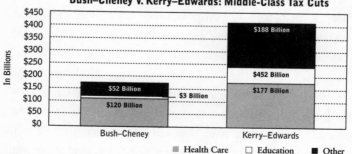

Bush–Cheney v. Kerry–Edwards: Middle-Class Tax Cuts

Office of Management and Budget, FY 2005; Kerry–Edwards Campaign

Even as we work to ease the squeeze, we will make sure to protect middle-class families that have been driven into debt by the combination of lagging incomes and climbing costs. We will crack down on unfair credit card and mortgage lending practices that make personal debt far worse, cost families their homes, and drive working people toward bankruptcy.

A strong economy requires trust in our economy. Investors need to trust that their money is being managed honestly and in their best interests. Workers need to trust that their pensions are secure. And consumers need to trust the products they buy. The great majority of chief executive officers are hardworking and honest, but we have seen what happens when a few corporations break the rules and break the trust of their shareholders and workers. We will work for corporate responsibility to increase transparency and protect the rights of investors and workers.

We will also fight to ensure that our legal system is working to establish the rules and incentives that are needed for the economy to function—without wasting time or money. One way we punish wrongdoing and deter misconduct is through our courts. Our courts—and in particular, the juries of regular citizens at their heart—play a central role in making sure that even the most powerful interests are held accountable, and even the most vulnerable people have protections. At the same time, there is no question that abuses of our legal system have hurt companies and individuals who are acting responsibly.

Frivolous malpractice lawsuits and class actions waste good people's time and money. That is wrong, and we support reforms that prevent and punish these abuses—while at the same time preserving the principles of responsibility and fairness that make our system work.

Our plan is not just aimed at strengthening families in the middle class; we are deeply committed to helping families *join* the middle class. The great middle-class expansion of the 1990s—that lifted our entire economy with it—has been reversed. Three million families have fallen into poverty under President Bush; in many states, welfare rolls are beginning to rise again after being cut in half during the late 1990s. It is time to turn that around so all people who work hard and meet their responsibilities have the chance to lift themselves out of poverty and into the middle class. Our plan will:

★ *Raise the minimum wage to $7.00 an hour by 2007. At this minimum wage a family of four with a full-time worker would no longer be forced to raise their children in poverty,*

★ *Increase tax credits for child care, an essential ingredient in ensuring the continued success of work-based welfare reform,*

★ *Defend and strengthen the Earned Income Tax Credit (EITC), increasing the reward to work for the most hard-pressed families and lifting millions out of poverty,*

★ *Invest in programs like Youthbuild that educate and prepare disadvantaged young people for jobs,*

★ *Encourage more women and minorities to pursue degrees in math and science, which lead to high paying jobs,*

★ *Invest in lifelong learning so that workers of all skill levels can access education and training to move up to better, higher paying jobs,*

★ *Encourage entrepreneurship in all our communities through initiatives like the New Markets venture capital initiative.*

★

RAISING THE MINIMUM WAGE
IS A WORKING WOMEN'S ISSUE

The minimum wage is a working women's issue. Women make up only 48 percent of the overall American workforce, but 61 percent of the people who will get a raise when we increase the minimum wage. People who live on the minimum wage do not get cost of living adjustments—every year that their costs climb but the minimum wage stays the same is another year people living on the minimum wage can afford less. Economists believe that the primary reason the wage gap expanded between middle- and low-wage women in the 1980s was the erosion in the minimum wage.

Our proposal to increase the minimum wage will especially help working mothers. There are 1.4 million working mothers who will get a direct raise, and another 3 million who could be helped. This will help mothers lift their families out of poverty and put more food on the table. Increasing the minimum wage to $7 would raise the annual earnings of a full-time worker by about $3,800 a year—enough for a low-income family to pay for ten months of groceries; eight months of rent; or a year's tuition at community college and an entire year of health care expenses.

★

If we are going to have a strong economy, we do not have a person to waste. Discrimination should never get in the way of accomplishment. We need to enforce civil rights laws that bar employers from discriminating based on skin color or disability, and we need new protections, like one banning on-the-job discrimination based on sexual orientation. We need to unleash the potential of America, from our inner cities to our rural farmlands. We must restore overtime protections for American workers, and strengthen the right to organize. Achieving our potential as a country means making the most of everyone's potential as an American.

We also need to start giving parents the tools they need to live up to their responsibilities. The 1996 welfare reform law focused on helping custodial parents—usually mothers—move from welfare to work. But we know that children do better when they have *two* involved parents, not just one. Today many parents are struggling with the job of raising children and at the same time face fewer opportunities and higher costs of child care, health care, and education. We will offer greater opportunities and job training to parents and in return, they will be required to fulfill their responsibilities to their children, including child support. That way we can strengthen families and communities at the same time.

We have an ironclad commitment to America's middle-class families. We know that the strong America of the 20th century was built by the great American middle class and all those who worked to join it. We understand that a strong America today means a strong and growing middle class.

We will champion middle-class interests and put middle-class values at the heart of all that we do. We pledge to honor work over wealth, and opportunity over privilege. We will lead America into a real responsibility era, by asking those at the top to do right by their companies and their workers; by challenging Americans to do right by their families, their communities, and their country; and by insisting that Washington balance its books and do right by the taxpayers for a change. We will fight for proven economic policies that bring prosperity to all Americans against discredited ideological theories that only help those who are already successful. We will lift middle-class incomes and cut middle-class taxes. And we will hold Washington strictly accountable for the impact of its policies on the American families that are our most important economic resource.

INVESTING IN TOMORROW'S ECONOMY

One of President Bush's economic advisors once memorably said: "Computer chips, potato chips, what difference does it make what we produce?" That attitude is sadly typical of the Bush administration's attitude toward the information-age economy, which depends on key public investments and policies aimed at spurring research and innovation.

Our plan will help America's innovators and entrepreneurs maintain our edge in tomorrow's economy through two major avenues.

The first is support for basic scientific research. We will:

★ *Boost the research budgets at the National Institutes of Health, the National Science Foundation, NASA and the*

Department of Energy, all of which have lost critical research resources during the Bush administration,

★ *Support the Advanced Technology Program which helps finance high-potential projects that struggle to obtain private-sector financing,*

★ *Extend the Research and Development Tax Credit for private R&D efforts,*

★ *Restore the scientific integrity of federal science review panels, which the Bush administration has often stacked with political appointees,*

★ *Invest aggressively in biotechnology research, where huge breakthroughs affecting human health, agricultural production, and new industrial projects are already visible on the horizon,*

★ *Reverse the Bush administration's ban on federally supported stem cell research which could soon produce cures for a variety of lethal chronic diseases, including diabetes, Parkinson's Disease, and cancer.*

★

AN OPEN LETTER TO THE AMERICAN PEOPLE

Signed by 48 Nobel Laureates, June 21, 2004

Presidential elections present us with choices about our nation's future. We support John Kerry for president and urge you to join us.

The prosperity, health, environment, and security of Americans depend on presidential leadership to sustain our vibrant science and technology; to encourage education at home and attract talented scientists and engineers from abroad; and to nurture a business environment that transforms new knowledge into new opportunities for creating quality jobs and reaching shared goals.

President Bush and his administration are compromising our future on each of these counts. By reducing funding for scientific research, they are undermining the foundation of America's future. By setting unwarranted restrictions on stem cell research, they are impeding medical advances. By employing inappropriate immigration practices, they are turning critical scientific talent away from our shores. And by ignoring scientific consensus on critical issues such as global warming, they are threatening the earth's future. Unlike previous administrations, Republican and Democratic alike, the Bush administration has ignored unbiased scientific advice in the policy-making that is so important to our collective welfare.

John Kerry will change all this. He will support strong investments in science and technology as he restores fiscal responsibility. He will stimulate the development and deployment of technologies to meet our economic, energy, environmental, health, and security needs. He will recreate an America that provides opportunity to all at home or abroad who can help us make progress together.

John Kerry will restore science to its appropriate place in government and bring it back into the White House. He is the clear choice for America's next president.

★

We will redouble our nation's commitment to closing the "digital divide" and expanding the digital economy, which will continue to transform how we work, communicate, shop, and relax, creating jobs and opportunity in the process. Our plan will:

★ *Make broadband universally accessible by providing tax credits for rural and underserved areas and the next generation of high-speed broadband,*

★ *Provide broadband to all first responders by the end of 2006,*

★ *Take action to "can spam" and ensure online privacy to grow the digital economy,*

★ *Support efforts to create "digital signatures" that will make e-commerce vastly more secure and convenient.*

★

INVESTING IN BROADBAND
IS AN INVESTMENT IN AMERICA'S FUTURE

Over the past four years, the United States has dropped from 4th to 10th in broadband use. Countries such as South Korea and Japan are now deploying networks that are 20 to 50 times faster than what is available in the United States. This administration's short-sighted economic plan does not promote the competition, innovation, and investment necessary to ensure high-speed data transmission, video-on demand, and interactive delivery services are available to all Americans.

Government research at the Defense Advanced Research Projects Agency (DARPA) led to the creation of the Internet and the government has an important but temporary role to play in catalyzing the extension of broadband to our entire nation.

It is especially important in creating new opportunities in areas of America—especially rural areas and some of our inner cities—that are now all but cut off from the economy of tomorrow. The same Internet technologies that make it possible to export technology and services jobs to India can make it possible to create similar jobs in rural areas here in America, which often enjoy a combination of low business costs and high quality of life.

Economists at the Brookings Institution have estimated that advancing the transition to high-speed broadband will expand the economy by $500 billion, including benefits for consumers and producers. Another researcher has estimated that a national high-speed broadband network would create 1.2 million jobs, including high-skill, high-wage jobs in communications and manufacturing.

Expanding high-speed broadband is the information-age equivalent of the rural electrification initiatives of the Roosevelt years: a strategic public investment that could pay off a thousand times over in creating new economic opportunities and spreading opportunity throughout our population. It is an investment opportunity that we literally cannot afford to pass up.

★

Building a strong economy starts with world-class education and training.

Today, Americans compete with workers on every continent. Information flows across oceans. High-wage jobs are more dependent than ever on high-level skills. In America, 60,000 engineers graduate a year—about one-tenth the number produced by India and China. No wonder we are falling behind in the competition for high-skill jobs.

Like no time in history, a good job requires a good education and good skills. A competitive workforce is an educated workforce. In the global economy, education pays.

That is why our strategy to build a strong economy includes a detailed plan to reform education in America—from preschool to graduate school. Our plan will keep the federal government's bargain with America's schools to leave no child behind; it will throw open the doors of college like never before by making it more affordable; it will encourage students to become scientists and engineers; and it will make sure every person willing to work hard has the chance to learn the skills he or she needs to succeed in today's economy.

★

LEE IACOCCA:
WHY JOHN KERRY IS BETTER FOR BUSINESS

Lee Iacocca is one of America's most respected can-do leaders. He made his career responding to a changing world. When foreign automakers were out-competing Americans in the 1980s, Lee Iacocca sent profits soaring after he introduced a spacious, family vehicle that no other automaker wanted to take a chance on: the minivan.

Even though he endorsed George W. Bush in 2000, Lee Iacocca believes John Kerry is the best choice in this election to lead America through the challenges we face ahead.

"I've met privately with John Kerry, I've talked with him, I read all his position papers, and I would suggest you do likewise. I like him. And I'm endorsing him to be our next president because I like what he says about get-ting every American a fair shot at a secure, well-paying job so they can provide for their families and enjoy life a little more," he said at an event in San Jose in June.

"John Kerry would make a great commander-in-chief, I have no doubt about that. He would also make one hell of a CEO. That's what a president is.

"He knows how to surround himself with good peo-ple, and he knows how to set priorities. He's a doer. And he does know how to make a tough decision now and then, believe me.

"We need a leader who is really dedicated to creat-ing millions of high-paying jobs all across the country. The bottom line is simple: we need a new CEO and president."

★

Our plan to build a strong economy is broad and ambi-tious, but also specific and responsible. It is based on proven strategies, but it is adapted to today's challenges. It offers a clear and specific alternative to the poor eco-nomic record and missing economic plan of President Bush. But most of all, we offer it in the sure knowledge that America's best, strongest, most prosperous days lie ahead. All we have to do is return to a path shaped by the enduring values of America: opportunity, responsibil-ity, honesty, fair play, and great rewards for hard work. That is how we give all our people the chance to succeed. That is how we keep on building the America we believe in. That is how we keep the promise of America.

CHAPTER THREE

★

FAMILY

We can build an America with strong,

healthy families where quality

health care and world-class education

are affordable and available

to every American.

John Kerry

★

A World-Class Education for All

Family is the center of everyday American life. Our parents are our first protectors, first teachers, first role models, and first friends. Parents know that America's great reward is the quiet but incomparable satisfaction that comes from building their families a better life. Strong families, blessed with American opportunity, guided by personal faith, and filled with American dreams are the heart of a strong America.

We believe that a strong America begins at home with strong families, and that we can help empower parents to build strong families.

The simple bargain at the heart of the American Dream offers opportunity to every American who takes the responsibility to make the most of it. And that bargain is the great source of American strength, because it unleashes the amazing talent and determination of our people. As our people seize the opportunity to build a better life, they build a stronger country.

Now, like never before, education is the key to that opportunity, essential to a strong America. We believe in an America that offers the best education to all our children— wherever they live, whatever their background. Period.

That means:

★ *Every child comes to school ready to learn,*

★ *Every student is held to high standards, and every school has the resources and responsibility to meet those standards,*

★ *Every classroom has a great teacher, and every student gets enough personal attention to foster a talent and help with a difficulty,*

★ *Every teenager expects to graduate from high school with a meaningful diploma,*

★ *Every qualified young person who wants to go to college can afford it,*

★ *Every adult who needs additional job training can get it.*

Today our government ignores the shameful truth that the quality of a child's education depends on the wealth of that child's neighborhood. Our best public schools are the best schools in the world, but too many children go to schools that just do not work. Too many children who beat the odds and succeed in school cannot afford to go on to college. And too many adults who need additional training are not able to get it.

In this White House, education is an easy promise—easy come, and easy go. When President Bush signed the No Child Left Behind Act, he said the right things—he asked more from our schools and pledged to give them the resources to get the job done. And then he promptly broke his word, providing schools $27 billion less than he had promised, literally leaving millions of children behind. Over the last four years, college tuitions have risen by 35 percent, pricing 220,000 students out of college. Yet President Bush tried to cut financial aid for 84,000 students.

We believe that a strong America begins at home with strong families, and that strong families need the best schools. We believe schools must teach fundamental skills like math and science, and fundamental values like citizenship and responsibility. We believe providing resources without reform is a waste of money, and reform without resources is a waste of time. And we believe leaders who expect students to learn responsibility should start by keeping their own promises.

Our plan for investing in the education and skills of our people begins with a simple pledge: we will keep the federal government's promise to Leave No Child Behind.

We both voted for that landmark legislation, which created a new bargain with states and school districts: we will ask more from you, and we will make sure you have the resources to get the job done. The Bush administration has broken that promise; we will keep it.

But we also believe that No Child Left Behind is only the beginning. That is why we have offered a plan to finish the job of education reform.

Nothing has a bigger impact than a teacher on the quality of a child's education. We will make an intensive effort to put a great teacher in every classroom, starting with a new bargain: offering teachers more, and asking more in return. Our plan will:

★ *Raise teacher pay, especially in the schools and subjects where great teachers are in the shortest supply,*

★ *Improve mentoring, professional development, and new technology training for teachers, instead of leaving teachers to sink or swim,*

★ *Create rigorous new tests for new teachers,*

★ *Provide higher pay for teachers who have extra skills and excel in helping children learn,*

★ *Ensure fast, fair procedures for improving or removing teachers who do not perform well on the job, while preserving protections from arbitrary dismissal.*

Instead of pushing private school vouchers that funnel scarce dollars away from public schools, we will support innovations within the public school arena—smaller schools, single-sex schools, and most of all, charter public schools that give teachers, parents, civic organizations, and social entrepreneurs the chance to pursue educational excellence under a simple guideline: flexibility in exchange for tangible results.

We also need a national campaign to raise graduation rates. Today 3 in 10 young people do not finish high school—and that is true for half of Hispanics, African-Americans, and Native Americans. In America, that is just intolerable. We will keep better track of graduation rates to hold schools accountable for raising them. Working with colleges, community groups, and faith-based organizations, we will offer more tutoring and mentoring to kids at risk. And when big high schools are not working, we need to make them smaller so kids get the attention they deserve.

Our plan will invest in afterschool programs that give students extra help and give parents peace of mind. We will also rebuild schools that are falling apart.

We will expand access to college and make it more affordable. The centerpiece of our plan is a college opportunity tax cut for middle-class families and a new bargain with the states. We will:

★   *Offer a College Opportunity Tax Credit on $4,000 of
tuition for all four years of college that will dramatically
reduce college costs for millions of students, especially
those who pay their own way and can least afford
college now,*

★   *Simplify the student aid process, with shorter forms
and better information about how to get aid,*

★   *Offer states $10 billion for higher education, if they
will keep tuition increases in line with inflation for
the next two years,*

★   *Offer hundreds of thousands of young people the
opportunity to pay for college by serving our country for
two years. We will pay for that initiative by reforming
our student loan system—making sure that the profits
of banks are set by an auction in the marketplace, not by
lobbyists in Congress.*

★

PROVIDING OPPORTUNITY THROUGH SERVICE:
JOHN KERRY AND YOUTHBUILD

"One of my proudest achievements as a senator is the
YouthBuild program. In 1991 I visited a YouthBuild program
and was deeply impressed by the young people I met and the
impact the program had on their lives. When I wrote the legislation that provided the funding for the national YouthBuild
program, I knew that it was a wonderful program that had
the potential to help young people, but over the years I have
been amazed by how successful the program has been and the
difference it has made in the lives of young people.

94

YouthBuild is the only national program that gives young adults the chance to contribute to their community through housing construction and the opportunity to learn basic education toward a diploma, learn skills training toward a decent paying job, develop leadership, find adult mentors and participate in a supportive community. Over the past ten years, 25,000 young people have produced over 10,000 unites of low-income housing. Burnt-out shells and abandoned buildings have come to life as attractive homes in communities where there's a critical need for housing. And at the same time that YouthBuild is turning around communities, it is turning around lives. Because what the students are building is not just houses, but a better future for themselves and their families."

—*John Kerry*

★

Getting into college is one thing; getting a degree is another. Today almost 50 percent of college freshmen do not graduate, and more than 60 percent of minorities never wear a cap and gown. We will strengthen preparation for college by expanding the GEAR-UP program to reach 2 million children a year. We will work with states to establish a more rigorous high school curriculum—one that prepares students for college or for higher-paying jobs. And we will create a small but strategic College Completion Fund that rewards colleges for graduating more of the students who have the highest risk of dropping out.

Nothing is more important to America's economic success today than our excellence in math and science.

But America is losing the math and science race. Less

than one-third of American students are "proficient" in math and science, according to the National Assessment of Educational Progress, and even at top universities, 20 percent of math classes are at a remedial level. As we mentioned, America graduates one-tenth the number of engineers produced by India and China. And fewer than 30 percent of scientists and engineers are female, African Americans, or Hispanic. If women and minorities joined fields like computer science, engineering, and physical science in proportion to their share of the total population, those shortages would be virtually eliminated. We will boost the number of scientists and engineers our colleges and universities produce.

Our plan will:

★ *Improve math and science teaching in our high schools, by giving teachers special training and partnering schools with colleges and science-based businesses,*

★ *Double National Science Foundation scholarships for graduate studies in math, science, and engineering,*

★ *Create a national campaign to attract women and minorities into math and science studies beginning in middle school, with innovations that include girls-only science and math schools, specialized afterschool programs, summer camps, and innovative ideas championed by leaders like Sally Ride, America's first female astronaut.*

Balancing work and family.

We believe that helping parents balance their work and family obligations is vital to building strong families. Today, most married families are working 12 hours more than in 1977. That means 12 hours less time to spend helping their kids with homework after school, eating dinner, or going to the ballgame. About 1 in 3 middle school students care for themselves after school, hours during which students are more likely to encounter drugs, alcohol and gangs.

We will help parents by expanding afterschool opportunities to another 2 million children, through a "School's Open 'Til 6" plan that meets the needs of working parents and focuses on good transportation to high-quality afterschool programs.

We will also help parents afford high-quality child care. High-quality early care and education are critical to success in school, the ability to have good relationships, and healthy development. Since 2000, child care costs have risen at twice the rate of inflation. We will raise the child care tax credit and ensure the credit benefits moderate-income families by making it partially refundable. And we will allow stay-at-home parents of infants to receive support from the tax credit.

We believe that churches and faith-based institutions play in important role in supporting strong families and strong communities. We will encourage these vital institutions to continue to play the role they have always played—as leaders, teachers, and guides in our communities. We will support faith-based efforts, including providing financial support, in a way that honors our Constitution and civil rights laws, and in a way that values the role of faith in building stronger families and communities.

★

Affordable Health Care for All Americans

We believe not just that a strong America begins at home, but that a strong America begins *in* the home. And just as government's first responsibility is the health and safety of its people, parents' first responsibility is the health and safety of their children.

But today, a family's ability to ensure that all its members get the quality health care they deserve is challenged like never before. America has the best health care system in the world—for those who can afford it. But tens of millions of Americans pay too much and get too little from our health care system, and tens of millions more have no health insurance at all.

Roughly 44 million Americans have no health insurance at all. More than 80 million Americans went without health care coverage at some point during the last two years. Even those with heath care coverage have seen costs soar dramatically—health insurance has increased by more than $2,600 for the typical family over the last three years. When that is combined with a $1,500 loss in income for the average family, it is obvious that middle-class families are being squeezed.

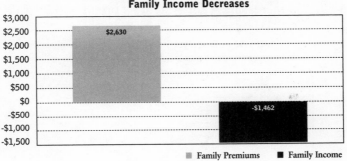

[Kaiser Family Foundation; Census Bureau]

Skyrocketing health care costs not only hurt our families—they hurt our economy. Small businesses cannot expand because they cannot afford to provide health coverage for their employees. Bigger businesses have trouble competing in the global economy because of the high cost of health care. Raises that workers need and deserve are swallowed by rising insurance premiums.

But the Bush administration has put drug companies and HMO profits above family health and small business costs. Total health care costs increased four times as fast as wages in the last year alone. Prescription drug spending has more than doubled during the past five years. Rising health care costs have forced businesses to slow hiring and shift jobs to part-time and temporary workers, many of whom lack health insurance. Yet the president has no plan to address any of these challenges. The few proposals he has offered would actually make the health care crisis worse by further dividing the system between one that is affordable for the healthy and wealthy, and one that is unaffordable for the elderly, the sick, and increasingly, for America's broad middle class.

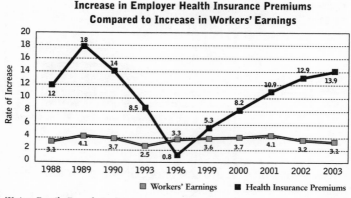

Increase in Employer Health Insurance Premiums Compared to Increase in Workers' Earnings

[Kaiser Family Foundation]

Families and businesses across the country are struggling to pay for rising health care costs. We have met people like John and Mary Ann Knowles. John lost his job a year and a half ago, and Mary Ann has breast cancer. And even while she is undergoing chemotherapy, she still has to go to work every day—just to hang onto their health insurance. That is the story of millions of Americans.

We believe that America can and must do better, and we are going to attack the health care crisis with a thorough and comprehensive approach. Our goal is simple: quality, affordable health coverage for all Americans to keep our families healthy, our businesses competitive, and our country strong.

Affordable and accessible health care for all Americans.

It is morally wrong to tolerate an America with so many uninsured and underinsured Americans. Working Americans who do not have health insurance live in the neighborhoods we call home. We see them every day behind the counter and around the corner. They build America's houses, run our small businesses, bag our groceries, and care for our elderly and our kids. And some American families, more than others, tend to fall through the cracks of our health care coverage system:

★ *Employees who work for small businesses that cannot afford to provide health insurance,*

★ *Middle-class families whose breadwinners are between jobs,*

★ *Self-employed Americans, independent contractors, and part-time or temporary workers who cannot get coverage from their employers and cannot afford to buy coverage on their own,*

★ *People near, but not at, the age where Medicare becomes available, who often cannot get affordable private health insurance. This is even more likely for those who lose their jobs, retire early, or suffer from chronic diseases, such as diabetes.*

But no matter why people are uninsured, the consequences can be devastating. The uninsured are more likely to file bankruptcy because of mounting health care bills, less likely to get regular checkups, and less likely to detect a disease in its early and most treatable forms. And it is also a serious economic problem. When some Americans do not have health care, all Americans pay the cost. Americans who do not have health insurance often do not get the preventive care they need. When they get sick, they go to emergency rooms and the bill is paid by other patients or taxpayers. In 2004, Americans are expected to pay $41 billion dollars for this "uncompensated care," with state and local governments, and taxpayers, paying the most.

A health care plan for every child.

A strong, healthy nation starts with healthy children.

Every parent knows the fear of waking up to the cries of a sick baby or a child with an ear infection that will not go away. As parents, we both remember the countless times we called that first pediatrician to get answers to every last question.

But far too many parents have another fear, on top of their child's health. They worry that a sick child means financial ruin. There are more than eight million uninsured children in our nation. These children are less likely to get a routine checkup, or to get treatment for common ailments like asthma. They miss more days of school. It is a disgrace that eight million children lack health insurance in the richest nation on earth.

Our plan starts by providing health insurance for every child in America. Under the Kerry-Edwards plan, the federal government will pay the full costs for the 20 million children in the Medicaid program. In return, we will ask states to expand coverage to children in families with higher incomes than are currently eligible, as well as low-income adults. This plan will expand coverage to millions of people and provide much needed relief for states that are struggling under persistent growing budgetary pressures.

The plan will also simplify the health care system so we can prevent children from falling through the cracks. Right now, there are millions of kids who are eligible for federal-state health insurance programs but are not signed up. There are lots of reasons—sometimes the enrollment forms require the skills of an accountant to figure out. Some states make parents sign up every six months in person, making it virtually impossible for a parent who cannot get time off or afford to lose a whole day of work. Some parents do not even know these programs are available.

Under our plan, kids will be signed up automatically at hospitals, community health centers, and schools. And $5 billion in enrollment bonuses will be available to states as an incentive to find uninsured children and keep them covered. Children do not choose their parents. They do not choose whether to have health insurance. Children deserve a good start—with both high quality education and health care. Under our plan, every child in America will have health insurance, and every parent will have a little more peace of mind.

Giving all Americans access to the same quality health care offered to Congress.

Too many people who do not have employer-based coverage do not have access to affordable health insurance. A recent study found that only one in ten applicants who need health care in the individual market can get insurance that is affordable and meets their medical needs.

Small businesses often face the same challenge. Without the buying power of a large corporation, they have a hard time getting high-quality, affordable health plans for their employees.

That is why our approach gives every American the right to buy the same coverage that Members of Congress give themselves. This is good coverage at a reasonable cost, with plenty of choices among private plans.

In addition to guaranteeing access to the Congressional Health Plan for all Americans, we will provide additional help for those who need the most help:

★ *Americans between the ages of 55 and 64 years old often have the hardest time finding an affordable health plan, because they tend to have more expensive health needs. Our plan provides millions of low and moderate income Americans in this age group with a 25 percent tax credit to help pay the cost of their premiums,*

★ *Americans who are between jobs often cannot afford health insurance, and some of them are not eligible for any plan at all. Our plan helps low and moderate income Americans between jobs by offering them a 75 percent tax credit to help pay for their premiums,*

★ *Small business employees are far less likely to have health insurance than employees of large business because health insurers tend to charge small businesses higher premiums for the same coverage. We will make health care more affordable for small businesses by offering them a tax credit that covers up to 50 percent of their premium contribution for low- to moderate-income employees,*

★ *Finally, low-to-moderate income individuals whose employers do not provide them with coverage will get a tax credit to help pay the cost of participating in the Congressional Health Plan.*

Under our plan, we will make sure that 95 percent of Americans, including all children, have health coverage. Our plan will provide health coverage for 27 million people who are currently uninsured.

Keeping down spiraling health costs.

At the center of our strategy to address the health care crisis is a plan to control spiraling health care costs. This is critical to keeping American businesses competitive in the world and for providing relief to middle class families who are being squeezed.

We have a public-private system that excels at innovation and has some of the best health care professionals in the world. But it is delivered by an enormous, low-tech bureaucracy—especially in the private sector—that soaks up $30 billion a year. That means that nearly one quarter of all our health care spending pays for preparing, submitting, calculating, paying, and collecting medical bills.

We lead the world in pharmaceutical research and development, but our products are often too expensive, especially for seniors who require costly drugs to treat chronic illnesses. So it is hard to understand how those same drugs—made by American companies—can be available for a fraction of the cost just over the border in Canada.

If left unchecked, the mounting cost crisis will result in a health care system that is the world's best for those who can afford it, and all but unreachable for those who cannot.

We have a plan to hold down costs, eliminate waste, and promote preventive care, better medicine, and disease management. These steps will improve the quality of health care and make it more affordable.

We will hold down health care premiums without relying on price controls or other outmoded approaches. We will begin by focusing on the largest driver of rising premiums: catastrophic health care costs. Health insurance claims for more than approximately $50,000 are less than one half of one percent of all claims—but they are 20 percent of medical expenses for private insurers. They boost premiums for everybody, bankrupt families with little or no insurance, and keep many small businesses from offering health coverage to their employees altogether.

Our plan offers employers a new bargain that will hold down costs and expand coverage. Under this bargain, the federal government will pick up 75 percent of the cost of catastrophic health claims for employers who agree:

★ *To provide quality coverage for their employees,*

★ *To share savings from lower premiums with their employees,*

★ *To adopt disease management programs and other incentives to improve overall employee health and reduce costs.*

This innovative plan will reduce a family's annual health care premiums by up to $1,000 and help expand employer-based coverage. At the same time, it will push the entire health care system toward better and more cost-effective medical practices. This proposal will also stabilize health care costs for businesses and insurance companies, and make those costs more predictable so businesses can improve their plans for the future.

We will improve the quality of care and enhance the efficiency of the medical system by cutting billions of wasted dollars in administrative processing and paperwork. As we mentioned, an astonishing 25 percent of total health care expenditures in the economy is spent on non-medical costs—mostly paperwork. Settling a single transaction in the health care system can cost as much as $25, while banks have cut their costs to less than a penny per transaction by using modern technology. If hospitals, doctors' offices, and health insurers use the same technologies now used throughout the rest of the private sector, they can radically reduce transaction costs. At the same time, they can expand use of medical best practices and reduce deadly medical errors.

All of this can—and must—occur in a system that rigorously protects patients' privacy. To promote an information-age revolution in our health care system, our plan will:

★ *Require private insurers who do business with the federal government—through programs like Medicare, Medicaid, and the Veterans Administration—to adopt advanced information systems to manage medical records and financial book-keeping,*

★ *Give health care providers bonuses for streamlining paperwork and using electronic medical record and billing systems,*

★ *Establish a goal to ensure that all Americans have secure, private medical records by 2008. This will not only cut costs, but eliminate unnecessary tests and drastically reduce medical errors.*

We are committed to affordable health care, and we are committed to quality health care. We will not accept one without the other.

A recent Institute of Medicine study found that between 44,000 and 98,000 people die of medical errors every year. The vast majority of injuries come not from negligent doctors or hospitals, but from outmoded practices, habits, and systems that are poorly designed to protect patients from errors. The gap between best practices and typical practices is extremely wide. We must close this gap for many chronic diseases, such as diabetes, stroke, congestive heart failure, and arthritis. Reducing the number of medical errors will save and improve tens of thousands of lives—and it will also save money that would otherwise be spent fixing mistakes.

★

REDUCING HEALTH CARE COSTS IS GOOD
FOR BUSINESS:

Rising health costs have played an important role in the job losses America has experienced in the last several years, especially in high-wage sectors like manufacturing. The large jump in health costs has led employers to either reduce their hiring or shift more workers to temporary or part-time jobs that do not have health benefits.

The largest job losses have been in the industries that have the best health benefits. For example, between 2000 and 2002 employment went down 13 percent for carmakers but went up 1 percent for car dealers. Part of the reason for this dramatic difference is health benefits. Automobile manufacturers get much more generous health benefits (total benefits are 25 percent of compensation) compared to auto dealers who get much less generous benefits (only 13 percent of compensation). In contrast, Canada has seen job growth across the board, including in manufacturing, in part because health costs do not vary across sectors.

Industry	Benefits as a Share of Total Compensation	Change in Employment 2000-02
Motor Vehicles (manufacturing)	25%	-13%
Primary Metals	20%	-19%
Construction	17%	0%
Car Dealers	13%	+1%
Food Service	11%	+4%

[Bureau of Economic Analysis]

Health care costs continue to drag down employment gains. Mark Zandi of Economy.com recently reported that the current trend of low-wage job growth is based on employers' unwillingness to hire employees with high-benefit packages. The high price of health care is pushing down the growth of high-paying, high-quality jobs.

★

The next part of our plan to reduce health care costs will improve the quality of care, reduce medical errors, and ensure healthier lives for all Americans by encouraging and rewarding disease management and prevention efforts. To reduce injuries and deaths from inadequate care, our plan would:

★ *Provide financial incentives to help providers and purchasers improve quality, including upfront capital investments for enhancing infrastructure in hospitals and other medical facilities,*

★ *Reward health care organizations and physicians with financial bonuses for investing in modern information systems,*

★ *Provide economic incentives to encourage the use of computers in prescribing medicine, because this can reduce medication errors by 80 percent or more,*

★ *Making medical errors transparent by changing the culture and habits in health care so that errors and patient injuries are immediately discovered and disclosed to prevent them from happening again.*

Finally, our plan will take steps to curb the rising cost of medical malpractice insurance, which not only raises overall health care costs but also threatens Americans' choice of providers in the health care system. Access to care is threatened as more providers are leaving their practices due to ever-increasing malpractice insurance premiums. Improvements can and should be made to our medical liability system. Lawsuits should be the last, not the first, line of defense. While we oppose arbitrary caps on malpractice suits that impose the biggest burdens on the victims wronged the most, our plan will reduce unnecessary mal-practice costs through five measures. We will:

★ *Oppose punitive damages except in cases where inten-tional misconduct, gross negligence, or reckless indiffer-ence to life can be established,*

★ *Require that individuals making medical malpractice claims first go before a qualified medical specialist to make sure a reasonable grievance exists,*

★ *Require states to ensure the availability of non-binding mediation in all malpractice claims before cases proceed to trial,*

★ *Support sanctions against plaintiffs and lawyers who bring frivolous medical malpractice claims, including a "three strikes and you're out" provision preventing lawyers who file three frivolous cases from bringing another suit for 10 years,*

★ *Eliminate the special privileges that allow insurance companies to fix prices and collude in ways that increase medical malpractice premiums.*

In the end, our plan to reduce health care costs focuses on applying 21st century efficiency to a system that has gone decades without real reform. Modernized medicine works better and costs less—we can increase health care quality while we decrease health care costs for families, employers, and government. And that is exactly what our plan will do.

Making prescription drugs affordable.

In the last year alone, prescription drug prices rose by 17 percent, four times the inflation rate.

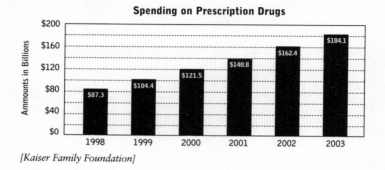

Spending on Prescription Drugs

[Kaiser Family Foundation]

The Medicare prescription drug benefit enacted by Congress last year was long-overdue recognition that prescription drugs are central to modern health care, especially in managing the chronic illnesses of so many seniors. But the new benefit is too costly, too complex, and woefully inadequate for seniors. It is no wonder a majority of seniors have refused to get the new drug discount cards. Despite much Bush administration election-year hoopla, price discounts have already been outstripped by rising prices. Many drugs in high-demand—like Lipitor, Prevacid, and Zocor—cost more with the new discount cards than they cost on the Internet. The unfortunate truth is that the real beneficiaries of the Bush prescription drug benefit are the drug companies and HMOs that have been guaranteed what is essentially an open-ended corporate subsidy.

Drug companies should make a profit in return for their investment in the research and development that produce

life-saving drugs and other critical medicine. But we oppose
anti-competitive policies that force American seniors to pay
excessive prices on new drugs and prevent Americans from
accessing cheaper generic and imported drugs.

	Prices under Medicare Savings Card		Current Prices without Savings Card	
Drug	Pharmacy Care Alliance	RxSavings	Drugstore.com	Federal Supply Schedule
Lipitor (10mg, 30 cap)	$71.19	$74.72	$62.99	$40.10
Prevacid (30mg, 30 cap)	$130.68	$147.01	$120.99	$53.90
Zocor (40 mg, 30 tap)	$128.69	$124.32	$123.99	$69.27
Aricept (10 mg, 30 cap)	$139.11	$132.39	$127.99	$76.51

*["New Medicare Drug Cards Offer Few Discounts," Minority Staff, Committee
on Government Reform, U.S. House of Representatives, April 2004.]*

Our plan for prescription drugs for seniors will:

★ *Give Americans access to the discounts available in
Canada and other countries by allowing re-importation
of safe, FDA-approved prescription drugs,*

★ *End artificial barriers to the availability of less expensive
generic drugs,*

★ *Require the federal government to negotiate better prices
for prescription drugs through programs like Medicare,*

★ *Demand disclosure of real costs and profits from the
pharmacy benefit managers who control drug benefits
for more than 200 million Americans under both public
and private health plans,*

★ *Give states incentives to negotiate better drug prices for participants in Medicaid and state employee health plans,*

★ *Overhaul the new Medicare drug benefit to ensure that seniors are not forced into HMOs.*

Protecting seniors' health care.

We are committed to guaranteeing quality health care for seniors, offering them real options for health coverage, and ensuring that they have access to affordable long-term care.

Our plan will:

★ *Ensure quality care throughout Medicare in every part of the country,*

★ *Give seniors a meaningful choice in health plans, and not coerce them into HMOs,*

★ *Ensure quality nursing home care with adequate inspections, faster reimbursements, and better training for nursing home workers,*

★ *Oppose efforts to abandon the national commitment to long-term care by cutting Medicaid or forcing states to take over key aspects of the program,*

★ *Let Medicaid pay for home and community-based care options,*

★ *Give caregivers involved in long-term care greater access to information, training, respite and counseling services.*

Passing a Patients' Bill of Rights.

We will enact a real Patients' Bill of Rights to put doctors and nurses back in charge of making medical decisions with their patients—instead of allowing HMO bureaucrats to make medical decisions. Americans deserve the right to choose their own doctor and have access to the specialists they want to see.

Along with Senator Edward Kennedy and Senator John McCain, we successfully fought to pass a Patients' Bill of Rights through the Senate for the first time in history. President Bush has blocked this bipartisan effort again and again. The Bush administration has even gone to the Supreme Court to take the side of HMOs against patients—preventing patients from suing an HMO that has wrongfully denied them the medical care they need. We will push for a real Patients' Bill of Rights that holds HMOs accountable for decisions that harm patients. We will also protect patients by guaranteeing:

★ *A right to see the specialists they need,*

★ *A right to real emergency protections,*

★ *A real external appeals process that allows patients to appeal an HMO decision,*

★ *Whistleblower protections that allow health care workers to report quality problems without fear of retaliation.*

Investing in science to battle disease.

Americans deserve access to the best information about illnesses and potential medical therapies and cures. We must look to the future with hope and confidence that advances in medicine will advance our best values. From working toward therapies for AIDS to working toward a cure for cancer, America has always been a land of discovery—of distant horizons and unconquered frontiers.

As part of that discovery, we must reverse the Bush administration's restrictions on embryonic stem cell research—supported by people from Nancy Reagan to Christopher Reeve to Michael J. Fox. We must make the funding of stem cell research a priority in our universities and our medical community, while ensuring strict ethical guidelines. More than 100 million Americans could potentially benefit from this research, including those suffering from Parkinson's, diabetes, and cancer. Part of our nation's greatness lies in our leadership of great medical discoveries, with our breakthroughs and our beliefs going hand-in-hand. If we pursue the limitless potential of our science—and trust that we can use it wisely—we will save millions of lives and ease human suffering.

Helping vulnerable Americans.

Many of us have friends, family, co-workers, or neighbors who struggle with a mental illness. We are committed to ending discrimination against Americans with mental illnesses and ensuring equal treatment for mental illness in our health system.

We must also fight to ensure that people with disabilities can meet their potential and participate fully in the American Dream. Our vision is for an America that ensures freedom, independence, and choices for people with disabilities. Part of that vision includes ensuring access to affordable health coverage and removing barriers to work. While we have made great strides by helping people with disabilities return to work without losing their health care, it is time to make sure that parents caring for children with disabilities can keep their jobs without worrying about paying their kids' health care bills. We will work to ensure that no one is kept in a nursing home or institution if they prefer to live elsewhere and can do so with the dignity they deserve.

We must also address the unjust disparities in our health care system—disparities often based on the color of a person's skin. Whether African Americans, Latinos, Asian Americans or Native Americans, the fact is that minorities continue to live less healthy lives and die younger in America. African Americans are one-third more likely than all other Americans to die from cancer. They have the highest rate of hypertension in the world. Latinos have the least insurance, with one in three having no coverage at all. Native Americans struggle with what can only be called the epidemic of diabetes, with rates near 50 percent in certain tribes. Tremendous gains in science and medicine have benefited millions of our citizens, but too often they are out of reach for minorities. We will work to eliminate these health disparities. From expanding health insurance to 95 percent of Americans, including for all our children, to improving language access programs in medical facilities, to ensuring access to quality care through greater disease management and prevention efforts, the time is now to improve the health of those Americans who have been left behind because of the color of their skin.

Moreover, our health care system has left behind too many of our nation's heroes. We must honor veterans' service by making sure they have access to medical services. Returning soldiers should have the care they need to treat wounds they received defending our country. In order to renew America's promise to its veterans, we will:

★ *Fight for mandatory funding for veterans health care,*

★ *Streamline the process so that veterans hear in a timely manner about their status and their benefits,*

★ *End fully and immediately the "disabled veterans tax," under which military retirees who receive both veterans' pensions and disability compensation must surrender a dollar from their military retirement pay for every dollar they get for disability compensation,*

★ *Support legislation to provide access to TRICARE, the military's health care system, for all members of the National Guard and Reserves.*

Our goal, and our plan, is to make the best medicine the standard for our health care system, and to make the best of our health care system available and affordable for every American. We believe in an America where every family looks to the future with hope and excitement, without worry that the cost of caring for its loved ones is too great to bear; where health care is a right, not a privilege; where strong, healthy families build a stronger America.

★

Conclusion: One America

Four years ago, President Bush promised the American people that he would be a uniter, not a divider—but he has been nothing of the sort.

He has sought political advantage in dividing people on matters of faith and conscience.

He has offered countless negative attacks against those who offer principled disagreement to his policies.

And his stubborn pursuit of a one-note economic strategy has allowed divisions of opportunity, once closing, to widen.

Today, some Americans have the best health care in the world. Yet more and more Americans find themselves unable to afford insurance for their children or the medicine they need.

Some Americans send their children to public schools that are among the best in the world. But too many others know that the buildings their children study in are falling down, and quality teachers are in terribly short supply. Very few Americans have reaped huge rewards from the president's tax cuts for those at the top. But most Americans are living on tighter and tighter budgets, often making less and definitely paying more than they did four years ago.

It does not have to be this way. And if the American people give us the chance to lead America in a new direction, it will not be this way.

Together, we will build one America.

One America—where every child has health insurance and the best health care is affordable for every individual.

One America—where all our children go to schools that their parents can be proud of, and that prepare them to build a great life.

One America—where all our people have the chance to prosper together; where the middle class is growing; where incomes are rising because work is honored—not just the wealth it creates; and where opportunity is a birthright that needs only responsibility to redeem.

One America—where all our people can be proud of the role we play in the world, and where people all around the world look to us for inspiration and with respect.

With your help, we will build one America—strong at home, respected in the world.

We will never pursue policies or allow tactics that exploit differences or encourage division. To the contrary, we will dedicate ourselves to building understanding and closing divides. And wherever there is intolerance or discrimination, we will be there to stand up and stand against it.

The America we believe in is not a divided nation.

The America we believe in is one great nation—built by people persecuted for their own beliefs; brought to life with a declaration that we are all created equal; and raised up by the courage of citizens in each successive generation determined to make our American Dream come true.

That is the America we are meant to be. That is the America we are fighting for. That is the America, with your help, we will build.

★ ★ ★

Clockwise from top:

July 7, 2004
*John Kerry and John Edwards
are cheered on by thousands in
Dayton, OH during the second stop
on their first campaign swing together.*

July 10, 2004
*Senators John Kerry and John Edwards
share a laugh while tossing a football
around on an Albuquerque, NM tarmac as
their campaign plane stood nearby.*

Clockwise from top:

July 6, 2004
*Senator John Kerry and wife Teresa Heinz Kerry
share a smile while peering out into the Market
Square crowd in Pittsburgh, PA just moments after
Senator Kerry named John Edwards to the ticket.*

June 6, 2004
*John Kerry greets Veterans at the University of
Minnesota, Minneapolis during a rally to mark the formal
rollout of the National Veterans for Kerry Campaign.*

May 7, 2004
*John Kerry greets a veteran during a campaign
stop in Louisiana. He is greeted by veterans as
he touches down in every state in the nation.*

Clockwise from top:

January 14, 2004
*John Kerry address potential caucus
goer in Iowa as Iowa Attorney General
Tom Miller looks on (far left) just days
before the Iowa caucuses.*

July 7, 2004
*Senators Kerry and Edwards share
a private moment in Pittsburgh before
going out on the campaign trail
together for the first time.*

Clockwise from top:

January 24, 2004
*John Kerry skates with former
professional hockey players
during a campaign stop at
the University of New Hampshire
just days before the primary.*

June 26, 2004
*John Kerry speaks to the National
Association of Latino Elected and
Appointed Officials in Washington DC.*

Clockwise from top:

June 16, 2004
John Kerry colors with a girl at the Marion Franklin Community Center in Columbus, OH on a day where he talked with Columbus families about his plan to stop the middle class squeeze.

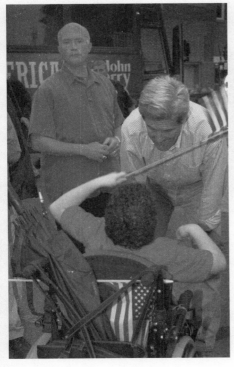

January 24, 2004
John Kerry, former professional hockey players and Kerry's youngest fans recite the pledge of allegiance before playing hockey in New Hampshire just days before the state's primary.

July 3, 2004
John Kerry visits with a supporter in Wisconsin during a campaign stop on his "Celebrating the Spirit of America" tour.

May 20, 2004
*John Kerry embraces
Representative Mike
Honda (D-CA) while
meeting with Asian
American leaders at
Kerry's DC headquarters.*

June 26, 2004
*A supporter looks on as
Senator Kerry addresses
the National Association
of Latino Elected and
Appointed Officials in
Washington, DC.*

Clockwise from top:

July 15, 2004
*John Kerry addresses Philadelphia residents
at the home of Bill and Mary Kay Bowden during
his "Front Porch Tour: Hometown Values
for a Stronger America."*

May 10, 2004
*Senator Kerry converses with health care
workers in Edinborough, PA. Kerry shared his plan
to provide health care to 99% of all Americans.*

Clockwise from top:

June 29, 2004
Senator Kerry with Silvestre Herrera (center), a Medal of Honor winner for his service in France during WWII. Also pictured, fellow veteran Rick Leal, joins Kerry and Herrera at the National Council of La Raza in Phoenix, Arizona.

July 7, 2004
John Edwards works the crowd at a campaign rally in St. Petersburg, FL. This was one of his first joint appearances with Senator Kerry since joining the "New Team for a New America."

Clockwise from top:

July 3, 2004
John Kerry tours the Dejno family farm in Independence, WI during his "Celebrating the Spirit of America".

June 21, 2004
John Kerry greets Christopher Chappell as he delivers a speech on "An Innovative Economy" in Denver, CO. Kerry was endorsed by 40 Nobel Prize winning scientists at this event.

January 23, 2004
John Kerry answers questions from New Hampshire voters during a campaign stop just days before the primary. His mantra to every potential voter was 'grill me' and he stayed until every question was answered.

Clockwise from top:

January 24, 2004
*John Kerry, campaigning in Derry, NH
greets supporters at a restaurant just days
before the primary.*

June 29, 2004
*John Kerry meets with supporters
in Phoenix after speaking to the National
Council of La Raza.*

Counter-Clockwise
from top:

July 3, 2004
*Senator Kerry takes
a break from the
"Celebrating the Spirit
of America Tour" to
visit a trap shooting
range in Holmen, WI
where the sharp shooting
candidate hit almost
every clay target.*

July 6, 2004
*Moments after announcing Senator John Edwards
as his choice for Vice President from Market Square
in Pittsburgh, Senator John Kerry leaves the stage and
waves to supporters with wife, Teresa Heinz Kerry.*

Clockwise from top:

July 9, 2004
Teresa Heinz Kerry, wife of Democratic Presidential nominee Senator John Kerry addresses a group of women gathered in New York City to see the new campaign team. Elizabeth Edwards, wife of Democratic Vice Presidential nominee John Edwards looks on.

July 7, 2004
John Kerry addresses a crowd in St. Petersburg, FL during a multi-state swing to introduce the "New Team for a New America."

July 29, 2003
John Kerry strolls with an Iowa farmer while discussing the issues most important to family farm owners.

Clockwise from top:

June 25, 2004
John Kerry addresses thousands at his rally for America workers in Perry, OH. Sarah Bender stands at the podium.

July 10, 2004
John Kerry mingles with supporters during a rally in Raleigh, NC at Carolina State University.

May 14, 2004
Martin Ornelas-Quintero, Executive Director of LLEGO, and Dr. Marsha Martin, executive Director of Aids Action, talk with Senator Kerry after a meeting with national LGBT leaders.

Clockwise from top:

June 15, 2004
*John Kerry chats with Lynette Farmer of
Columbus, OH during a front porch visit.
Kerry and Edwards have done a series
of front porch tours bringing their
campaign and their vision for America
to everyday Americans.*

July 10, 2004
*Over 25,000 people gathered to welcome
John Edwards home as the running mate of
John Kerry at a welcoming rally at North
Carolina State University Raleigh.*

Clockwise from top:

June 15, 2004
John Kerry greets children during his Rally in the Park at a campaign stop in Columbus, OH.

July 4, 2004
John Kerry walks in Cascade, Iowa's 4th of July parade during his "Celebrating the Spirit of America" tour of the heartland.

Clockwise from top:

July 6, 2004
*The families of John Kerry and John Edwards
tour the Rosemont farm in Pittsburgh, PA
on their first full day as campaign partners.*

July 7, 2004
*The Kerry's and the Edwards' share a fun
moment on stage in St. Petersburg, Florida on
their first campaign swing together.*

December 31, 2003
*John Kerry with Franklin LaMere aboard
the "Real Deal Express" bus during a campaign
swing during Sioux City, IA last year.*

July 3, 2004
*John Kerry, on the road
in Wisconsin during his
"Celebrating the Spirit
of America" tour waves
to onlookers from his
campaign bus.*

Section Two

Table of Contents

★

★

Speech to the
2004 Democratic National Convention
Remarks of Senator John Kerry

I'm John Kerry and I'm reporting for duty.

We are here tonight because we love our country.

We are proud of what America is and what it can become.

My fellow Americans, we are here tonight united in one simple purpose: to make America stronger at home and respected in the world.

A great American novelist wrote that you can't go home again. He could not have imagined this evening. Tonight, I am home. Home where my public life began and those who made it possible live. Home where our nation's history was written in blood, idealism, and hope. Home where my parents showed me the values of family, faith, and country.

Thank you, all of you, for a welcome home I will never forget.

I wish my parents could share this moment. They

went to their rest in the last few years, but their example, their inspiration, their gift of open eyes, open mind, and endless world are bigger and more lasting than any words.

I was born in Colorado, in Fitzsimons Army Hospital, when my dad was a pilot in World War II. Now, I'm not one to read into things, but guess which wing of the hospital the maternity ward was in? I'm not making this up. I was born in the West Wing!

My mother was the rock of our family as so many mothers are. She stayed up late to help me do my homework. She sat by my bed when I was sick, and she answered the questions of a child who, like all children, found the world full of wonders and mysteries.

She was my den mother when I was a Cub Scout and she was so proud of her fifty-year pin as a Girl Scout leader. She gave me her passion for the environment. She taught me to see trees as the cathedrals of nature. And by the power of her example, she showed me that we can and must finish the march toward full equality for all women in our country.

My dad did the things that a boy remembers. He gave me my first model airplane, my first baseball mitt, and my first bicycle. He also taught me that we are here for something bigger than ourselves; he lived out the responsibilities and sacrifices of the greatest generation to whom we owe so much.

When I was a young man, he was in the State

Department, stationed in Berlin when it and the world were divided between democracy and communism. I have unforgettable memories of being a kid mesmerized by the British, French, and American troops, each of them guarding their own part of the city, and Russians standing guard on the stark line separating East from West. On one occasion, I rode my bike into Soviet East Berlin. And when I proudly told my dad, he promptly grounded me.

But what I learned has stayed with me for a lifetime. I saw how different life was on different sides of the same city. I saw the fear in the eyes of people who were not free. I saw the gratitude of people toward the United States for all that we had done. I felt goose bumps as I got off a military train and heard the Army band strike up "Stars and Stripes Forever." I learned what it meant to be America at our best. I learned the pride of our freedom. And I am determined now to restore that pride to all who look to America.

Mine were greatest generation parents. And as I thank them, we all join together to thank that whole generation for making America strong, for winning World War II, winning the Cold War, and for the great gift of service which brought America fifty years of peace and prosperity.

My parents inspired me to serve, and when I was a junior in high school, John Kennedy called my generation to service. It was the beginning of a great journey—

a time to march for civil rights, for voting rights, for the environment, for women, and for peace. We believed we could change the world. And you know what? We did.

But we're not finished. The journey isn't complete. The march isn't over. The promise isn't perfected. Tonight, we're setting out again. And together, we're going to write the next great chapter of America's story.

We have it in our power to change the world again. But only if we're true to our ideals—and that starts by telling the truth to the American people. That is my first pledge to you tonight. As President, I will restore trust and credibility to the White House.

I ask you to judge me by my record: As a young prosecutor, I fought for victim's rights and made prosecuting violence against women a priority. When I came to the Senate, I broke with many in my own party to vote for a balanced budget, because I thought it was the right thing to do. I fought to put a 100,000 cops on the street.

And then I reached across the aisle to work with John McCain, to find the truth about our POW's missing in action, and to finally make peace with Vietnam.

I will be a commander in chief who will never mislead us into war. I will have a Vice President who will not conduct secret meetings with polluters to rewrite our environmental laws. I will have a Secretary of Defense who will listen to the best advice of our military leaders. And I will appoint an Attorney General who actually upholds the Constitution of the United States.

My fellow Americans, this is the most important election of our lifetime. The stakes are high. We are a nation at war—a global war on terror against an enemy unlike any we have ever known before. And here at home, wages are falling, health care costs are rising, and our great middle class is shrinking. People are working weekends; they're working two jobs, three jobs, and they're still not getting ahead.

We're told that outsourcing jobs is good for America. We're told that new jobs that pay $9,000 less than the jobs that have been lost is the best we can do. They say this is the best economy we've ever had. And they say that anyone who thinks otherwise is a pessimist. Well, here is our answer: There is nothing more pessimistic than saying America can't do better.

We can do better and we will. We're the optimists. For us, this is a country of the future. We're the can-do people. And let's not forget what we did in the 1990s. We balanced the budget. We paid down the debt. We created 23 million new jobs. We lifted millions out of poverty and we lifted the standard of living for the middle class. We just need to believe in ourselves—and we can do it again.

So tonight, in the city where America's freedom began, only a few blocks from where the sons and daughters of liberty gave birth to our nation—here tonight, on behalf of a new birth of freedom—on behalf of the middle class who deserve a champion, and those struggling to join it who deserve a fair shot—for the brave men and women in uniform who risk their lives every day and the families who pray for their return—for all those who believe our best days are ahead of us—for all of you—with great faith in the American people, I accept your nomination for President of the United States.

I am proud that at my side will be a running mate whose life is the story of the American dream and who's worked every day to make that dream real for all Americans—Senator John Edwards of North Carolina. And his wonderful wife Elizabeth and their family. This son of a mill worker is ready to lead—and next January, Americans will be proud to have a fighter for the middle class to succeed Dick Cheney as Vice President of the United States.

And what can I say about Teresa? She has the strongest moral compass of anyone I know. She's down to earth, nurturing, courageous, wise and smart. She speaks her mind and she speaks the truth, and I love her for that, too. And that's why America will embrace her as the next First Lady of the United States.

For Teresa and me, no matter what the future holds or the past has given us, nothing will ever mean as much as our children. We love them not just for who they are and what they've become, but for being themselves, making us laugh, holding our feet to the fire, and never letting me get away with anything. Thank you, Andre, Alex, Chris, Vanessa, and John.

And in this journey, I am accompanied by an extraordinary band of brothers led by that American hero, a patriot named Max Cleland. Our band of brothers doesn't march together because of who we are as veterans, but because of what we learned as soldiers. We fought for this nation because we loved it and we came back with the deep belief that every day is extra. We may be a little older now, we may be a little grayer, but we still know how to fight for our country.

And standing with us in that fight are those who shared with me the long season of the primary campaign: Carol Moseley Braun, General Wesley Clark, Howard Dean, Dick Gephardt, Bob Graham, Dennis Kucinich, Joe Lieberman, and Al Sharpton.

To all of you, I say thank you for teaching me and testing me—but mostly, we say thank you for standing up for our country and giving us the unity to move America forward.

My fellow Americans, the world tonight is very different from the world of four years ago. But I believe the American people are more than equal to the challenge.

Remember the hours after September 11th, when we came together as one to answer the attack against our homeland. We drew strength when our firefighters ran up the stairs and risked their lives, so that others might live. When rescuers rushed into smoke and fire at the Pentagon. When the men and women of Flight 93 sacrificed themselves to save our nation's Capitol. When flags were hanging from front porches all across America, and strangers became friends. It was the worst day we have ever seen, but it brought out the best in all of us.

I am proud that after September 11th all our people rallied to President Bush's call for unity to meet the danger. There were no Democrats. There were no Republicans. There were only Americans. How we wish it had stayed that way.

Now I know there are those who criticize me for seeing complexities—and I do—because some issues just aren't all that simple. Saying there are weapons of mass destruction in Iraq doesn't make it so. Saying we can fight a war on the cheap doesn't make it so. And proclaiming mission accomplished certainly doesn't make it so.

As President, I will ask hard questions and demand hard evidence. I will immediately reform the intelligence system—so policy is guided by facts, and facts are never distorted by politics. And as President, I will bring back this nation's time-honored tradition: the United States of America never goes to war because we want to, we only go to war because we have to.

I know what kids go through when they are carrying an M-16 in a dangerous place and they can't tell friend from foe. I know what they go through when they're out on patrol at night and they don't know what's coming around the next bend. I know what it's like to write letters home telling your family that everything's all right when you're not sure that's true.

As President, I will wage this war with the lessons I learned in war. Before you go to battle, you have to be able to look a parent in the eye and truthfully say: "I tried everything possible to avoid sending your son or daughter into harm's way. But we had no choice. We had to protect the American people, fundamental American values from a threat that was real and imminent." So lesson one, this is the only justification for going to war.

And on my first day in office, I will send a message to every man and woman in our armed forces: You will never be asked to fight a war without a plan to win the peace.

I know what we have to do in Iraq. We need a President who has the credibility to bring our allies to our side and share the burden, reduce the cost to American taxpayers, and reduce the risk to American soldiers. That's the right way to get the job done and bring our troops home.

Here is the reality: that won't happen until we have a president who restores America's respect and leadership—so we don't have to go it alone in the world.

And we need to rebuild our alliances, so we can get the terrorists before they get us.

I defended this country as a young man and I will defend it as President. Let there be no mistake: I will never hesitate to use force when it is required. Any attack will be met with a swift and certain response. I will never give any nation or international institution a veto over our national security. And I will build a stronger American military.

We will add 40,000 active duty troops—not in Iraq, but to strengthen American forces that are now overstretched, overextended, and under pressure. We will double our special forces to conduct anti-terrorist operations. We will provide our troops with the newest weapons and technology to save their lives—and win the battle. And we will end the backdoor draft of National Guard and reservists.

To all who serve in our armed forces today, I say, help is on the way.

As President, I will fight a smarter, more effective war on terror. We will deploy every tool in our arsenal: our economic as well as our military might; our principles as well as our firepower.

In these dangerous days there is a right way and a wrong way to be strong. Strength is more than tough words. After decades of experience in national security, I know the reach of our power and I know the power of our ideals.

We need to make America once again a beacon in the world. We need to be looked up to and not just feared.

We need to lead a global effort against nuclear proliferation—to keep the most dangerous weapons in the world out of the most dangerous hands in the world.

We need a strong military and we need to lead

strong alliances. And then, with confidence and determination, we will be able to tell the terrorists: You will lose and we will win. The future doesn't belong to fear; it belongs to freedom.

And the front lines of this battle are not just far away—they're right here on our shores, at our airports, and potentially in any town or city. Today, our national security begins with homeland security. The 9-11 Commission has given us a path to follow, endorsed by Democrats, Republicans, and the 9-11 families. As President, I will not evade or equivocate; I will immediately implement the recommendations of that commission. We shouldn't be letting 95 percent of container ships come into our ports without ever being physically inspected. We shouldn't be leaving our nuclear and chemical plants without enough protection. And we shouldn't be opening firehouses in Baghdad and closing them down in the United States of America.

And tonight, we have an important message for those who question the patriotism of Americans who offer a better direction for our country. Before wrapping themselves in the flag and shutting their eyes and ears to the truth, they should remember what America is really all about. They should remember the great idea of freedom for which so many have given their lives. Our purpose now is to reclaim democracy itself. We are here to affirm that when Americans stand up and speak their minds and say America can do better, that is not a challenge to patriotism; it is the heart and soul of patriotism.

You see that flag up there. We call her Old Glory. The stars and stripes forever. I fought under that flag, as did so many of you here and all across our country. That flag flew from the gun turret right behind my head. It was shot through and through and tattered, but it never ceased to wave in the wind. It draped the caskets of men I served with and friends I grew up with. For us, that flag is the most powerful symbol of who we are and what we believe in. Our strength. Our diversity. Our love of country. All that makes America both great and good.

That flag doesn't belong to any president. It doesn't belong to any ideology and it doesn't belong to any political party. It belongs to all the American people.

My fellow citizens, elections are about choices. And choices are about values. In the end, it's not just policies and programs that matter; the president who sits at that desk must be guided by principle.

For four years, we've heard a lot of talk about values. But values spoken without actions taken are just slogans. Values are not just words. They're what we live by. They're about the causes we champion and the people we fight for. And it is time for those who talk about family values to start valuing families.

You don't value families by kicking kids out of after school programs and taking cops off our streets, so that Enron can get another tax break.

We believe in the family value of caring for our children and protecting the neighborhoods where they walk and play.

And that is the choice in this election.

You don't value families by denying real prescription drug coverage to seniors, so big drug companies can get another windfall.

We believe in the family value expressed in one of the oldest Commandments: "Honor thy father and thy mother." As President, I will not privatize Social Security. I will not cut benefits. And together, we will make sure that senior citizens never have to cut their pills in half because they can't afford life-saving medicine.

And that is the choice in this election.

You don't value families if you force them to take up a collection to buy body armor for a son or daughter in the service, if you deny veterans health care, or if you tell middle class families to wait for a tax cut, so that the wealthiest among us can get even more.

We believe in the value of doing what's right for everyone in the American family.

And that is the choice in this election.

We believe that what matters most is not narrow appeals masquerading as values, but the shared values that show the true face of America. Not narrow appeals that divide us, but shared values that unite us. Family and faith. Hard work and responsibility. Opportunity for all—so that every child, every parent, every worker has an equal shot at living up to their God-given potential.

What does it mean in America today when Dave McCune, a steel worker I met in Canton, Ohio, saw his job sent overseas and the equipment in his factory literally unbolted, crated up, and shipped thousands of miles away along with that job? What does it mean when workers I've met had to train their foreign replacements?

America can do better. So tonight we say: Help is on the way.

What does it mean when Mary Ann Knowles, a woman with breast cancer I met in New Hampshire, had to keep working day after day right through her chemotherapy, no matter how sick she felt, because she was terrified of losing her family's health insurance?

America can do better. And help is on the way.

What does it mean when Deborah Kromins from Philadelphia, Pennsylvania, works and saves all her life only to find out that her pension has disappeared into thin air—and the executive who looted it has bailed out on a golden parachute?

America can do better. And help is on the way.

What does it mean when 25 percent of the children in Harlem have asthma because of air pollution?

America can do better. And help is on the way.

What does it mean when people are huddled in blankets in the cold, sleeping in Lafayette Park on the doorstep of the White House itself—and the number of families living in poverty has risen by three million in the last four years?

America can do better. And help is on the way.

And so we come here tonight to ask: Where is the conscience of our country?

I'll tell you where it is: it's in rural and small town America; it's in urban neighborhoods and suburban main streets; it's alive in the people I've met in every part of this land. It's bursting in the hearts of Americans who are determined to give our country back its values and its truth.

We value jobs that pay you more not less than you earned before. We value jobs where, when you put in a week's work, you can actually pay your bills, provide for your children, and lift up the quality of your life. We value an America where the middle class is not being squeezed, but doing better.

So here is our economic plan to build a stronger America:

First, new incentives to revitalize manufacturing.

Second, investment in technology and innovation that will create the good-paying jobs of the future.

Third, close the tax loopholes that reward companies for shipping our jobs overseas. Instead, we will reward companies that create and keep good paying jobs where they belong—in the good old U.S.A.

We value an America that exports products, not jobs—and we believe American workers should never have to subsidize the loss of their own job.

Next, we will trade and compete in the world. But

our plan calls for a fair playing field—because if you give the American worker a fair playing field, there's nobody in the world the American worker can't compete against.

And we're going to return to fiscal responsibility because it is the foundation of our economic strength. Our plan will cut the deficit in half in four years by ending tax giveaways that are nothing more than corporate welfare—and will make government live by the rule that every family has to follow: pay as you go.

And let me tell you what we won't do: we won't raise taxes on the middle class. You've heard a lot of false charges about this in recent months. So let me say straight out what I will do as President: I will cut middle class taxes. I will reduce the tax burden on small business. And I will roll back the tax cuts for the wealthiest individuals who make over $200,000 a year, so we can invest in job creation, health care, and education.

Our education plan for a stronger America sets high standards and demands accountability from parents, teachers, and schools. It provides for smaller class sizes and treats teachers like the professionals they are. And it gives a tax credit to families for each and every year of college.

When I was a prosecutor, I met young kids who were in trouble, abandoned by adults. And as President, I am determined that we stop being a nation content to spend $50,000 a year to keep a young person in prison for the rest of their life—when we could invest $10,000 to give them Head Start, Early Start, Smart Start, the best possible start in life.

And we value health care that's affordable and accessible for all Americans.

Since 2000, four million people have lost their health insurance. Millions more are struggling to afford it.

You know what's happening. Your premiums, your co-payments, your deductibles have all gone through the roof.

Our health care plan for a stronger America cracks down on the waste, greed, and abuse in our health care system and will save families up to $1,000 a year on their premiums. You'll get to pick your own doctor—and patients and doctors, not insurance company bureaucrats, will make medical decisions. Under our plan, Medicare will negotiate lower drug prices for seniors. And all Americans will be able to buy less expensive prescription drugs from countries like Canada.

The story of people struggling for health care is the story of so many Americans. But you know what, it's not the story of senators and members of Congress. Because we give ourselves great health care and you get the bill. Well, I'm here to say, your family's health care is just as important as any politician's in Washington, D.C.

And when I'm President, America will stop being the only advanced nation in the world which fails to understand that health care is not a privilege for the wealthy, the connected, and the elected—it is a right for all Americans.

We value an America that controls its own destiny because it's finally and forever independent of Mideast oil. What does it mean for our economy and our national security when we only have 3 percent of the world's oil reserves, yet we rely on foreign countries for 53 percent of what we consume?

I want an America that relies on its own ingenuity and innovation—not the Saudi royal family.

And our energy plan for a stronger America will invest in new technologies and alternative fuels and the cars of the future—so that no young American in uniform will ever be held hostage to our dependence on oil from the Middle East.

I've told you about our plans for the economy, for education, for health care, for energy independence. I want you to know more about them. So now I'm going to say something that Franklin Roosevelt could never have said in his acceptance speech: go to johnkerry.com.

I want to address these next words directly to President George W. Bush: In the weeks ahead, let's be optimists, not just opponents. Let's build unity in the American family, not angry division. Let's honor this nation's diversity; let's respect one another; and let's never misuse for political purposes the most precious document in American history, the Constitution of the United States.

My friends, the high road may be harder, but it

leads to a better place. And that's why Republicans and Democrats must make this election a contest of big ideas, not small-minded attacks. This is our time to reject the kind of politics calculated to divide race from race, group from group, region from region. Maybe some just see us divided into red states and blue states, but I see us as one America—red, white, and blue. And when I am President, the government I lead will enlist people of talent, Republicans as well as Democrats, to find the common ground—so that no one who has something to contribute will be left on the sidelines.

And let me say it plainly: in that cause, and in this campaign, we welcome people of faith. America is not us and them. I think of what Ron Reagan said of his father a few weeks ago, and I want to say this to you tonight: I don't wear my own faith on my sleeve. But faith has given me values and hope to live by, from Vietnam to this day, from Sunday to Sunday. I don't want to claim that God is on our side. As Abraham Lincoln told us, I want to pray humbly that we are on God's side. And whatever our faith, one belief should bind us all: The measure of our character is our willingness to give of ourselves for others and for our country.

These aren't Democratic values. These aren't Republican values. They're American values. We believe in them. They're who we are. And if we honor them, if we believe in ourselves, we can build an America that's stronger at home and respected in the world.

So much promise stretches before us. Americans have always reached for the impossible, looked to the next horizon, and asked: What if?

Two young bicycle mechanics from Dayton asked, what if this airplane could take off at Kitty Hawk? It did that and changed the world forever. A young president asked, what if we could go to the moon in ten years? And now we're exploring the solar system and the stars themselves. A young generation of entrepreneurs asked, what if we could take all the information in a library and put it on a little chip the size of a fingernail? We did and that too changed the world forever.

And now it's our time to ask: What if?

What if we find a breakthrough to cure Parkinson's, diabetes, Alzheimer's, and AIDS? What if we have a president who believes in science, so we can unleash the wonders of discovery like stem cell research to treat illness and save millions of lives?

What if we do what adults should do—and make sure all our children are safe in the afternoons after school? And what if we have a leadership that's as good as the American dream—so that bigotry and hatred never again steal the hope and future of any American?

I learned a lot about these values on that gunboat patrolling the Mekong Delta with young Americans who came from places as different as Iowa and Oregon, Arkansas, Florida, and California. No one cared where we went to school. No one cared about our race or our backgrounds. We were literally all in the same boat. We looked out, one for the other—and we still do.

That is the kind of America I will lead as President—an America where we are all in the same boat.

Never has there been a more urgent moment for Americans to step up and define ourselves. I will work my heart out. But, my fellow citizens, the outcome is in your hands more than mine.

It is time to reach for the next dream. It is time to look to the next horizon. For America, the hope is there. The sun is rising. Our best days are still to come.

Goodnight, God bless you, and God bless America.

★

Speech to the
2004 Democratic National Convention
Remarks of Senator John Edwards

Thank you. Now, you know why [my wife] Elizabeth is so amazing.

I am a lucky man: to have the love of my life at my side. We have been blessed with four beautiful children: Wade, Cate, Emma Claire, and Jack.

My mother and father, Wallace and Bobbie Edwards, are here tonight. You taught me the values that I carry with me in my heart: faith, family, responsibility, and opportunity for everyone. You taught me that there's dignity and honor in a hard day's work. You taught me that you look out for your neighbors, you never look down on anybody, and you treat everyone with respect.

Those are the values John Kerry and I believe in, and nothing makes me prouder than standing with him in this campaign. I am so humbled to be your candidate for Vice President of the United States.

I want to talk about our next president. For those who want to know what kind of leader he'll be, I want to take you back about thirty years. When John Kerry graduated college, he volunteered for military service. He volunteered to go to Vietnam and to captain a swift boat, one of the most dangerous duties you could have. And as a result he was wounded and honored for his valor.

If you have any question about what he's made of, you need to spend three minutes with the men who served with him then and stand by him today.

They saw up close what he's made of. They saw him reach down and pull one of his men from the river and save his life. And in the heat of battle, they saw him decide in an instant to turn his boat around, drive it straight through an enemy position, and chase down the enemy to save his crew.

Decisive. Strong. Aren't these the traits you want in a Commander in Chief?

We hear a lot of talk about values. Where I come from, you don't judge someone's values based on how they use that word in a political ad. You judge their values based upon what they've spent their life doing.

So when a man volunteers to serve his country, and puts his life on the line for others—that's a man who represents real American values.

This is a man who is prepared to keep the American people safe and to make America stronger at home and respected in the world.

John is a man who knows the difference between what is right and what is wrong. He wants to serve you—your cause is his cause. And that is why we must and we will elect John Kerry as our next president.

For the last few months, John has been talking about his positive, optimistic vision for the country—talking about his plan to move this country in the right direction.

But we've seen relentless negative attacks against John. So in the weeks ahead, we know what's coming—don't we—more negative attacks.

Aren't you sick of it?

They are doing all they can to take this campaign for the highest office in the land down the lowest possible road.

This is where you come in. Between now and November—you, the American people—you can reject the tired, old, hateful, negative politics of the past. And instead you can embrace the politics of hope, the politics of what's possible because this is America, where everything is possible.

I am here tonight because I love my country. And I have every reason to love my country because I have grown up in the bright light of America.

I grew up in a small town in rural North Carolina. My father worked in a mill all his life, and I will never forget the men and women who worked with him. They had lint in their hair and grease on their faces. They worked hard and tried to put a little something away every week so their kids and their grandkids could have a better life. They are just like the autoworkers, office workers, teachers, and shopkeepers on Main Streets all across America.

My mother had a number of jobs. Her last job was working at the post office so my parents could have health care. And she owned her own small business—refinishing furniture to help pay for me go to college.

I have had such incredible opportunities in my life, and I was blessed to be the first person in my family to go to college. I worked my way through, and I have had opportunities way beyond what I could have ever imagined.

And the heart of this campaign—your campaign—is to make sure that everyone has those same opportunities that I had growing up—no matter where you live, who your family is, or what the color of your skin is. This is the America we believe in.

I have spent my life fighting for the kind of people I grew up with. For two decades, I stood with families and children against big HMOs and big insurance companies. And as a Senator, I fought those same fights against the Washington lobbyists and for causes like the Patients' Bill of Rights.

I stand here tonight ready to work with you and John to make America strong again.

And we have so much work to do. Because the truth is, we still live in two different Americas: one for people who have lived the American Dream and don't have to worry, and another for most Americans who work hard and still struggle to make ends meet.

It doesn't have to be that way. We can build one America.

We can build one America where we no longer have two healthcare systems. One for people who get the best healthcare money can buy and then one for everybody

else, rationed out by insurance companies, drug companies, and HMOs—millions of Americans who don't have
any health insurance at all.

It doesn't have to be that way.

We have a plan that will offer everyone the same
health care your Senator has. We can give tax breaks to
help pay for your health care. And we will sign into law
a real Patients' Bill of Rights so you can make your own
health care decisions.

We shouldn't have two public school systems in this
country: one for the most affluent communities, and one
for everybody else.

None of us believe that the quality of a child's education should be controlled by where they live or the affluence of their community.

It doesn't have to be that way.

We can build one public school system that works
for all our children. Our plan will reform our schools
and raise our standards. We can give our schools the
resources they need. We can provide incentives to put
quality teachers in the places and the subjects where we
need them the most. And we can ensure that three million kids have a safe place to go after school. This is what
we can do together.

We shouldn't have two different economies in
America: one for people who are set for life—their kids
and grandkids will be just fine—and then one for most
Americans who live paycheck to paycheck.

And you know what I'm saying. You don't need me
to explain it to you, you know—you can't save any

money, can you? Takes every dime you make just to pay your bills, and you know what happens if something goes wrong—a child gets sick, somebody gets laid off, or there's a financial problem. You go right off the cliff.

And what's the first thing to go? Your dreams.

It doesn't have to be that way.

We can strengthen and lift up your families. Your agenda is our agenda—so let me give you some specifics.

First, we can create good paying jobs in America again. Our plan will stop giving tax breaks to companies that outsource your jobs. Instead, we will give tax breaks to American companies that keep jobs here in America. And we will invest in the jobs of the future—in the technologies and innovation to ensure that America stays ahead of the competition.

We will do this because for us a job is about more than a paycheck—it's about dignity and self-respect. Hard work should be valued in this country and we're going to reward work, not just wealth.

We don't want people to just get by; we want people to get ahead. So let me give you some specifics about how we're going to do that.

To help you pay for health care, a tax break and health care reform to lower your premiums up to $1,000. To help you cover the rising costs of child care, a tax credit up to $1,000 to cover those costs so your kids have a safe place to go while you work. And to help your child have the same chance I had and be the first person in your family to go to college, a tax break on up to $4,000 in tuition.

So now you ask how are we going to pay for this? Well, here's how we're going to pay for it. Let me be very clear: for 98 percent of Americans, you will keep your tax cut—that's 98 percent. But we'll roll back the tax cuts for the wealthiest Americans, close corporate loopholes, and cut government contractors and wasteful spending. We can move our country forward without passing the bill and the burden on to our children and grandchildren.

We can also do something about 35 million Americans who live in poverty every day. Here's the reason we should not just talk about it, but do something about millions of Americans who still live in poverty, because it is wrong. We have a moral responsibility to lift those families up.

I mean the very idea that in a country of our wealth and our prosperity, we have children going to bed hungry. We have children who don't have the clothes to keep them warm. We have millions of Americans who work full-time every day for minimum wage to support their family and still live in poverty—it's wrong.

These are men and women who are living up to their part of the bargain: working hard and taking care of their families. Those families are doing their part; it's time we did ours.

We will do that when John is in the White House. We will raise the minimum wage, finish the job on welfare reform, and bring good paying jobs to the places that need them. And we will say no forever to any American working full-time and living in poverty—not in our America, not in our America.

Let me talk about why we need to build one America. I saw up close what having two Americas does to our country.

From the time I was very young, I saw the ugly face of segregation and discrimination. I saw young African-American kids sent upstairs in movie theaters. I saw white only signs on restaurant doors and luncheon counters. I feel such an enormous responsibility when it comes to issues of race and equality and civil rights.

I have heard some discussions and debates about where, and in front of what audiences we should talk about race, equality, and civil rights. Well, I have an answer to that question: everywhere.

This is not an African-American issue, not a Latino issue, not an Asian-American issue. This is an American issue. It's about who we are, what our values are, what kind of country we want to live in.

What John and I want—what we all want—is for our children and our grandchildren to be the first generations to grow up in an America that's no longer divided by race.

We must build one America. We must be one America, strong and united for another very important reason—because we are at war.

None of us will ever forget where we were on September 11th. We share the same terrible images: the Towers falling, the Pentagon in flames, and the smoldering field in Pennsylvania. And we share the profound sadness for the nearly three thousand lives lost.

As a member of the Senate Intelligence Committee, I know that we have to do more to fight terrorism and protect our country. And we can do that. We are approaching the third anniversary of September 11th, and I can tell you that when we're in office, it won't take us three years to get the reforms in our intelligence we need to protect our country. We will do whatever it takes, for as long as it takes, to make sure that never happens again, not to our America.

When John is president, we will listen to the wisdom of the September 11th Commission. We will build and lead strong alliances and safeguard and secure weapons of mass destruction. We will strengthen our homeland security and protect our ports, safeguard our chemical plants, and support our firefighters, police officers and EMT's. We will always use our military might to keep the American people safe.

And we will have one clear unmistakable message for al Qaeda and the rest of these terrorists: You cannot run. You cannot hide. And we will destroy you.

John understands personally about fighting in a war. And he knows what our brave men and women are going through in another war—the war in Iraq.

The human cost and extraordinary heroism of this war, it surrounds us. It surrounds us in our cities and towns. And we will win this war because of the strength and courage of our own people.

Some of our friends and neighbors saw their last images in Baghdad. Some took their last steps outside of Fallujah. And some buttoned their uniform for the final time before they went out to save their unit.

Men and women who used to take care of themselves, they now count on others to see them through the day. They need their mother to tie their shoe. Their husband to brush their hair. And their wife's arm to help them across the room.

The stars and stripes wave for them. The word hero was made for them. They are the best and the bravest. They will never be left behind. You understand that. And they deserve a president who understands on the most personal level what they have gone through—what they have given and what they have given up for their country.

To us, the real test of patriotism is how we treat the men and women who put their lives on the line every day to defend our values. And let me tell you, the 26 million veterans in this country won't have to wonder if they'll have health care next week or next year—they will have it always because they took care of us and we will take care of them.

But today, our great United States military is stretched thin. More than 140,000 are in Iraq. Nearly 20,000 are serving in Afghanistan. And I visited the men and women there and we're praying for them as they keep working to give that country hope.

Like all of those brave men and women, John put his life on the line for our country. He knows that when authority is given to the president, much is expected in return. That's why we will strengthen and modernize our military.

We will double our Special Forces, and invest in the new equipment and technologies so that our military remains the best equipped and best trained in the world. This will make our military stronger so we're able to defeat every enemy in this new world.

But we can't do this alone. We have to restore our respect in the world to bring our allies to us and with us. It's how we won the World Wars and the Cold War and it is how we will build a stable Iraq.

With a new president who strengthens and leads our alliances, we can get NATO to help secure Iraq. We can ensure that Iraq's neighbors like Syria and Iran, don't stand in the way of a democratic Iraq. We can help Iraq's economy by getting other countries to forgive their enormous debt and participate in the reconstruction. We can do this for the Iraqi people and our soldiers. And we will get this done right.

A new president will bring the world to our side, and with it, a stable Iraq and a real chance for peace and freedom in the Middle East, including a safe and secure Israel. And John and I will bring the world together to face our most dangerous threat: the possibility of terrorists getting their hands on a nuclear, chemical or biological weapon.

With our credibility restored, we can work with other nations to secure stockpiles of the world's most dangerous weapons and safeguard this dangerous material. We can finish the job and secure all loose nukes in Russia. And we can close the loophole in the Nuclear Nonproliferation Treaty that allows rogue nations access to the tools they need to develop these weapons.

That's how we can address the new threats we face. That's how we can keep you safe. That's how we can restore America's respect around the world.

And together, we will ensure that the image of America—the image all of us love—America this great shining light, this beacon of freedom, democracy, and human rights that the world looks up to—that that beacon is always lit.

The truth is every child, every family in America will be safer and more secure if you grow up in a world where America is once again looked up to and respected. That's the world we can create together.

Tonight, as we celebrate in this hall, somewhere in America, a mother sits at the kitchen table. She can't sleep. She's worried because she can't pay her bills. She's working hard to pay the rent and feed her kids. She's doing everything right, but she still can't get ahead.

It didn't use to be that way in her house. Her husband was called up in the Guard and he's been serving in Iraq for more than a year. She thought he'd be home last month, but now he's got to stay longer.

She thinks she's alone. But tonight in this hall and in your homes—you know what? She's got a lot of friends. We want her to know that we hear her. And it's time to bring opportunity and an equal chance to her door.

We're here to make America stronger at home so she can get ahead. And we're here to make America respected in the world so that we can bring him home and American soldiers don't have to fight the war in Iraq and the war on terror alone.

So when you return home, you might pass a mother on her way to work the late-shift—you tell her...hope is on the way.

When your brother calls and says that he's working all the time at the office and still can't get ahead—you tell him...hope is on the way.

When your parents call and tell you their medical bills are through the roof—you tell them...hope is on the way.

When your neighbor calls you and says that her daughter has worked hard and wants to go to college—you tell her...hope is on the way.

When you talk to your son or daughter who is serving this country and protecting our freedoms in Iraq—you tell them...hope is on the way.

And when you wake up and sit with your kids at the kitchen table, talking to them about the great possibilities in America, you make sure that they know that John and I believe at our core that tomorrow can be better than today.

Like all of us, I have learned a lot of lessons in my life. Two of the most important are that first, there will always be heartache and struggle—you can't make it go away. But the other is that people of good and strong will can make a difference. One lesson is a sad lesson and the other's inspiring. We are Americans and we choose to be inspired.

We choose hope over despair, possibilities over problems, optimism over cynicism. We choose to do what's right even when those around us say, "You can't do that." We choose to be inspired because we know that we can do better—because this is America where everything is still possible.

What we believe—what John Kerry and I believe—is that you should never look down on anybody, that we should lift people up. We don't believe in tearing people apart. We believe in bringing people together. What we believe—what I believe—is that the family you're born into and the color of your skin in our America should never control your destiny.

Join us in this cause. Let's make America stronger at home and respected in the world. Let's ensure that once again, in our one America—our one America—tomorrow will always be better than today.

Thank you and God bless you.

★

"Equal Justice and the Courts"
Remarks of Senator John Kerry at
the Drake Law School Supreme Court Celebration

We are here tonight to honor our next generation of lawyers and to honor your state's most esteemed jurists, the Iowa Supreme Court. It is a Supreme Court whose history is worthy of celebration. In 1868, the Iowa Supreme Court ruled that a girl could not be denied access to her neighborhood school because of the color of her skin. The very next year, this Court ruled that women could not be denied the right to practice law in Iowa. And in 1873, Iowa's high court ruled that an African American woman who was a passenger on a steamboat had the very same rights as the white passengers traveling with her.

These decisions were decades ahead of where most of our nation stood when it came to recognizing the rights of all Americans. I hope all of you take great pride in this legacy.

Thirty years ago this fall, I enrolled at Boston College Law School at a time when the nation at large was catching up to some of those early Iowa decisions. I went to law school as part of a generation at the crossroads. Vietnam had tested our faith in institutions and transformed so many of us into activists knocking on doors and raising our voices to hold the system accountable from the outside. We'd seen that the law could be an engine for progress, that barriers could be broken when idealistic citizens gave voice to our fundamental values inside a courtroom. We'd seen Attorney General Bobby Kennedy send the National Guard into hostile territory to face down Bull Connor and his snarling police dogs. We'd read of a brilliant young lawyer by the name of Thurgood Marshall, whose arguments in Brown v. Board of Education led the Supreme Court to strike down a false doctrine of "separate and unequal." We were marching for the ERA in the streets of New York, but we had faith that the law would respond to just impulses because Roe v. Wade had expanded the meaning of equality and freedom for all Americans.

I went to law school because I believed the struggle for justice I'd seen in the movement against the war could still be advanced in a courtroom. I still believed the law was a way to give power to those who had been denied it and to give a voice to the voiceless. I couldn't wait to put that belief to the test first as a student prosecutor working in the DA's office, and then as an assistant district attorney in Middlesex County, Massachusetts.

My faith in the law was reaffirmed. We modernized the district attorney's office and ended a backlog of thousands of cases to deliver justice on time. We took on criminals who preyed on the weakest and most vulnerable members of our society. We helped kids who were abused and neglected. We worked with police who needed to know that we had reformed and revitalized the justice system so the criminals they risked their lives to track down didn't fall through the cracks of a big bureaucracy.

And we helped create one of the nation's first rape crisis crime units—at a time when violence against women was a subject that was often swept under the rug. I remember speaking with the women who would come into our office. The terror they had experienced. The fear that was in their eyes. But most of all, I remember their dignity and determination in the face of the most terrible crimes. It's an every day reminder I carry around with me about why I must do everything in my power to support the rights of women and to take on the cowards that attack our mothers, sisters, and daughters.

I'm sure that many of the students who are graduating from this law school this year begin their legal career for idealistic reasons of their own. I applaud you and all your fellow students for your dedication to this important profession. Yet, as you no doubt know from your studies, you are beginning your legal careers in a very different era. Instead of paving the path of equality and freedom, too many recent court decisions have served as roadblocks.

Make no mistake, there are many, many wonderful judges sitting on the bench around the country and sitting in this room here tonight. They work every day in a legal system that is overburdened. They do their level best to implement our laws, make real our Constitution, and protect our rights. They are respected in their communities and sources of pride for our country.

Despite all that, I believe we cannot afford to ignore a disturbing trend in our judicial system. In the past three years, courts have struck down or weakened important sections of the Violence Against Women Act, the Americans with Disabilities Act, and the Age Discrimination in Employment Act. And they have continued to steadily erode the right to choose.

This change in the wind isn't just a natural swing of the pendulum, it isn't a coincidence, and it isn't an accident. It seems instead to be part of a process of politicization in our legal system. This process should concern all of us who look to the courts for justice and wisdom.

Drake Law School's Supreme Court competition was begun sixty-six years ago, in 1937, with the goal of fostering good relations between the school, the bench, and the bar. At that time, Americans feared that politicians were trying to subvert the independence of the courts. This concern is as important now as it was then. Our courts should never be wholly owned subsidiaries of one political party, one point of view, one ideology, or one president.

Last year, President Bush told an audience that, "We've got to get good, conservative judges appointed to the bench and approved by the United States Senate." With all due respect, I disagree. I don't believe we need conservative judges or liberal judges or anything but patriotic American judges who will enforce the laws and the Constitution of the United States.

Whenever one party attempts to turn judicial decisions into political debates, it causes Americans to doubt the independence of the courts and to question their role. But most importantly, it takes important issues out of the realm of legislation and executive actions—areas where the people, through their voice and their votes, can exert influence. Instead, crucial choices on policy matters are made by judges acting in a super-legislative capacity. In these instances, the quality of justice for all suffers. But those that suffer most, are those who most need protections and equality. This includes minorities, gays and lesbians. Tonight, I would like to focus my remarks on women and what the politicization of justice means to them and their lives.

Judicial nominees by the present administration have records that I believe are troubling to American women and those that support their equal rights. Judges like Charles Pickering and Priscilla Owen have long records of opposition to Roe v. Wade, have sought to restrict laws barring sexual discrimination, have supported a ban on interracial marriage, and have worked to narrow laws on gender discrimination. Nominations to the courts should not be occasions to advance partisan agendas but rather opportunities to advance justice.

I believe recent judicial decisions and nominations have made American women less safe and less secure—on the job and on the streets. And I believe our government and our legal system needs to be back on the side of women standing up for their security, ensuring their safety, supporting their rights, and guaranteeing their dignity. This nation can do no less.

I strongly feel that we do not need more judges that embrace the types of views that led the Supreme Court to recently strike down parts of the Americans with Disabilities Act—a landmark piece of bipartisan legislation that is the equivalent to the Civil Rights Bill to those with disabilities and the shining legacy of your great Senator, Tom Harkin. Unfortunately, the Court found that a nurse who had been demoted for missing work because of her breast cancer treatments could not hold her employers accountable for their actions under this act.

And this year, the Court is looking at potentially weakening the Family and Medical Leave Act. I have joined a brief to the Court arguing that this fundamental protection for American women and families should not be undermined.

Our legal system, of course, extends beyond the courts. Over the course of the past two years, Attorney General Ashcroft has presided over an unfortunate politicization of the Justice Department. Civil rights enforcement has been cut back and anti-domestic violence efforts have been eliminated.

But perhaps no decision better symbolizes what judicial politicization means for American women than the decision to strip down the Violence Against Women Act. This piece of legislation told America, "We will put the power of the federal government on the side of battered women who have had no voice." Bonnie Campbell, Iowa's former Attorney General, led the nation in recognizing the terrible toll of violence against women. All Americans owe her a debt of gratitude.

The Violence Against Women Act was passed by Republicans and Democrats alike. Not a single member of the House of Representatives voted against it. Yet, the right of women to sue their attackers in federal court was struck down.

And as if that weren't enough, Nancy Pfotenhauer, a strident opponent of the Violence Against Women Act, was appointed to the government body which is charged with guiding the Act's implementation. Pfotenhauer opposed the Violence Against Women Act when it was in Congress and supported the challenge to it at the Supreme Court. Talk about the fox guarding the chicken coop.

Pfotenhauer's organization even claims that "the battered women's movement has outlived its useful beginnings." With studies showing that one in five women will be victims of a rape or attempted rape in the course of their lifetime, I'd say that the fight to prevent violence against women is still in its useful beginnings. We have a long way to go.

I was proud to help lead the effort in 1994 to create specialized anti-domestic violence efforts through the COPS initiative. And we saw the number of domestic violence incidents drop by about twenty percent in four years. When that type of effort is completely eliminated, I believe it sets us on the wrong track.

We need to be concerned about the affirmative action initiatives which millions of American women depend on for justice and fairness. And we must safeguard Title Nine of the Civil Rights Act. Just last week, an administration commission on Title Nine came back with recommendations that would gut a law that has opened doors for millions of girls and young women. These recommendations have been rejected on a bipartisan basis and for good reason.

And finally there is the issue of choice. This issue is about the right of American women to control their own bodies, their own lives, and their own destinies. It is about their right to make their own decisions in consultation with their doctor, their conscience, and their God.

Anyone who has talked to or knows a woman who has faced this dilemma knows how difficult, how painful and how lonely it can be. We can't go back to the days of back alleys—days in which women were shamed by the high and mighty and forced to put their lives at risk. We can't put women in the place where their choice is to break the law and be branded a criminal. Women need access to information, to choices, and to their legal rights.

It won't surprise you to know I think that elections for Congress and the Presidency are important. But appointments to the bench are just as important— maybe more so. Senators and presidents come and go. Judges rule for a lifetime. Those of you in law school now could be dealing with the rulings of some of these new judges for most of your legal careers.

And while they only see a tiny percentage of federal cases, there is a reason the Supreme Court is the highest court in the land. It is there that debates are settled, that doctrines are set, and that millions of Americans look for justice and wisdom. In recent years, we have seen a court that has split five to four on important cases. With divisions so great, it is important that the next appointment to the Supreme Court be an individual who can bring consensus, not conflict. At a time of war, the American people have no stomach for another partisan confirmation battle. If a retirement opens up, our discussion should be an occasion to focus on the Constitution and what's right, not on confrontation and wrangling.

I believe we should work to expand the rights and opportunities for women and help make it is easier to be a good employee and a good parent. We should strengthen and restore the Violence Against Women Act and put the federal government foursquare on the side of women who have been threatened, endangered, and harmed.

We should improve the Family and Medical Leave Act to help even more Americans care for their children and their parents. Millions of Americans are struggling to do right by their children and often their aging parents. We need action to help them balance work and family.

We should protect Title Nine and its guarantee that women get a fair shake.

We should make sure that an equal days pay for an equal days work is a reality and not just a slogan.

And we must ensure that the right to choose is never abridged, never weakened, and never taken away.

Through the appointments that are made to important legal positions and through the actions we take, we will make the lives of American women stronger and more secure. Women deserve a government that honors and respects them as individuals and as citizens.

When we discuss laws and courts, judges and decisions, it is sometimes easy to forget what is really at stake. But at its heart, this issue is about more than marble columns and majority opinions, more than black robes and the black letter. It is about women like Christy Brzonkala. Christy was in the September of her first year at Virginia Tech when she stopped by the room of two men one night on her way home from a party. I won't go into the brutal details of what happened next, but it changed Christy's life forever. When she reported to the school that she had been raped, they dithered and then did nothing. So she took the men to court under the Violence Against Women Act. It was her case that the Supreme Court used to turn back that law. Christy and all the other women, and men, of this country look to the courts for justice and they deserve just that.

Supreme Court Justice Potter Stewart once said that, "The mark of a good judge is a judge whose opinion you can read and have no idea if the judge was a man or a woman, Republican or Democrat, a Christian or a Jew. You just know he or she was a good judge." Those are the kinds of judges we need in America once again. Judges who respect human dignity, protect our rights and liberties, believe in genuine equality. Judges who know that "Equal Justice Under the Law" isn't just an inscription, it's a promise. That is a promise that all of you who are here tonight from first year law students to Supreme Court Justices believe in. That is the type of justice—and the type of Justices—that all Americans deserve. Thank you.

★

Excerpts from

"A Lifetime of Service"

Remarks of Senator John Kerry at American Legion

September 11th, 2001, was a date that changed our history and our hearts. It was the most brutal and deadly attack America has ever known. We lost so many lives that morning: three thousand husbands and daughters, mothers and brothers, friends and heroes. And we lost long held illusions of invulnerability—the comfortable assumption of our geography that we were literally oceans away from conflict—that when and if we became involved, it was always "over there."

But then it happened here—and that has become a central fact of our time. Yet even as the buildings collapsed, even amidst the smoke rising from the ruins, it became clear that there was a deeper truth that could lift us and light our way: On that day—as in past days of peril and tragedy—we became one nation. One nation in spirit and resolve—and one nation in caring for one another. As heroes gave their lives on the steps of the World Trade Center and at the Pentagon trying to rescue and save, as hundreds lined up to give blood and thousands to volunteer, as help poured in from across the country and millions contributed to the families of the victims, we as a people offered the most powerful witness of our generation to our national character: Our greatest strength, and the highest duty of citizenship, is service.

...Nothing I hope to do as president will be more vital than reconnecting America's public life to the ideal of full citizenship. In this time of testing, of profound danger and vast potential, the real question we face is not what America can offer to us, but what each of us owe to America. To protect our nation and meet our potential, we will have to harness the faith, the energy, and the commitment of people of all ages in communities across the country.

Too often today, citizenship and duty are dismissed as peripheral or as fond memories of a forgotten past. But day after day, they are a way of life for millions. And they have sustained and strengthened our democracy for more than two centuries.

It was the sense of service and sacrifice that inspired a few Massachusetts farmers to leave their plows and stand up to the mightiest empire in the world at Lexington and Concord. It was to "that last full measure of devotion" that an American president paid immortal tribute on a cool November day in Gettysburg. It was that call to serve that led my father and the greatest generation to enlist in the Army Air Corps during World War II, that led a new generation to the frontlines in

Vietnam and then led many of the returning veterans to oppose that war when they came home.

In that same spirit, millions of Americans make a contribution and a difference every day—when they swear a Scout oath, help out in a hospital or homeless shelter, or tutor in a local school.

Visiting this nation more than a hundred fifty years ago, Alexis De Tocqueville observed that America is great because Americans are good. All over this country, Americans are demonstrating their fundamental goodness and decency to their fellow citizen and the world when they volunteer and serve. Washington doesn't have all the answers and government doesn't need to reinvent the wheel. What we can do is enhance local efforts, empower citizens to do what's right, and bring together government and businesses to leverage the great work that is being done by volunteers—in Boys and Girls Clubs, religious groups, and thousands of different places and projects all over America. Teachers transfer values, mentors transfer values, helpers and healers transfer values—and they deserve a government that's on their side in that important work.

More than any other nation, America is not just a place on the globe but an idea—and at the heart of that idea is a belief in the dignity and duty of every citizen—that all of us have something to give and each of us has a responsibility to serve.

For America, citizenship is not just a status or a slogan; it is the force that has forged our past and it must be the foundation of our future.

...Americans deserve a government that has as much faith in the ideals of America as they do. They deserve leaders for whom duty, honor, and responsibility are principles, not punch lines.

...We have seen before what happens when we appeal to the best instincts of America. Confined to his wheelchair, Franklin Roosevelt summoned Americans to stand tall against the tide of depression. Sixty years ago, his Civilian Conservation Corps sent millions of the young out to rebuild the nation even as they built a better life for themselves. John Kennedy called my generation to the Peace Corps—and Lyndon Johnson's VISTA opened up the chance to serve in the most forgotten places in our own land, valleys of deprivation and despair so often unseen and unheard. And then, ten years ago this month, President Clinton introduced AmeriCorps and inaugurated a new season of service.

Today, I propose not only to build on that tradition, but to go beyond it—because today, our challenges are different and our commitment must be even greater. We need a new era of service—not an effort for one time, one purpose, or one group—but a permanent and national endeavor. For America now, service is not just an option, but an obligation of citizenship.

...I learned about duty and obligation from my parents—through their words and by their example. My mother was a lifelong volunteer in our community and an environmental activist before the term even existed. My father was on the front end of the Greatest Generation. He set aside his career and volunteered even before America entered World War II. While he was off on duty, my mother sent him a letter. "You have no idea of the ways in which one can be useful right now," she wrote. "There's something for everyone to do."

Two decades later, Martin Luther King told us: "Everybody can be great because everybody can serve." Today America will be secure and strong if everybody does serve because there is work for all to do, a place for all to serve, and no room on the sidelines.

I see an America where every citizen of every age and background can make a difference and meet an obligation higher than themselves.

I see an America where, in a seamless web of service and concern, we offer Americans the challenge and the chance to do their duty—and Americans, in turn, step forward and give something back.

I see an America where in times of trouble and in triumph, of threat and hope, we ask not just what government can do, but what we can do.

It was my generation that in our youth heard that call—and I remember shortly afterwards my own period of service. We did not think we were special. We just thought we were doing our part. And in the end, I supposed that is all any of us can do—and I believe each of us must try.

I believe that a new army of American patriots stands ready for a new era of service. They only await a call to service that is certain and true. It is time to sound that call again. And that's why I am running for president. Thank you.

★

"A Return to Fiscal Responsibility"
Remarks of Senator John Kerry at Georgetown University

Before we begin today, I want to honor the sacrifice made by the brave American soldiers who gave their lives in Iraq over these last difficult days. Our prayers and our thoughts are with their families, and we will never forget their service for the country we love.

No matter our disagreements over how to approach policy in Iraq, we are all united as a nation in supporting our troops and ultimately in our goal of a stable Iraq.

When William Gaston, after whom this hall is named and this college's first student, arrived here in 1791, America was a young nation with a people yearning for freedom and opportunity. The promise of America was that the paths to a better life would be open to those who worked hard and planned for the future.

That is still the promise of the America we believe in and the America we must reclaim. And building an America in which middle-class incomes are rising, good jobs are being created, and working people can build a better life for their families is what this election is all about.

There is a fundamental difference in this election: President Bush has no real economic plan for long term prosperity and higher standards of living. I do—and at its heart is a strategy to create 10 million new jobs in the first term of a Kerry administration.

This president, whose tax cuts for the wealthiest Americans have left America 7 million jobs behind what he promised, now seems to think that one month when unemployment actually increased can make up for three years of massive job losses. He doesn't seem to know—or acknowledge—that the industries that are expanding pay an average of $9,000 less than ones that are contracting.

George Bush talks about a recovery, but doesn't seem to realize that today we have a wage recession in America—with average American workers making $1,200 less a year; with millions of families struggling to pay higher health care costs, higher property taxes and higher college tuitions—all of it out of lower incomes. While Americans are becoming more and more productive, they are increasingly working at lower wage jobs.

President Bush praises the productivity of our workers, but never mentions the unfairness which denies them the gains of their own labor.

Due to George Bush's tax cuts for the wealthiest Americans, the average worker now pays more in taxes at the local level. The burden for most Americans has gone up while wages have gone down.

By almost every measure of real life in the real America, George W. Bush just doesn't seem to understand what's happening to hard-working families.

So the great issue in this election is how to move America in a new direction.

And a strong America begins at home—with the state of our economy.

But instead of a credible economic plan and an honest debate, our present leadership has given us the old politics of false and simplistic negative attacks. I am committed to a different course.

Two weeks ago, in the first of a series of speeches, I set out my proposal to end tax benefits that encourage outsourcing and actually reward American companies for moving jobs overseas. Outsourcing will occur, but a company that stays here should not be put at a competitive disadvantage because a company that leaves can defer paying its taxes—perhaps forever. That's the law today; in fact, our taxpayers even spend $12 billion a year to subsidize the export of jobs. If I am president, I will fight to change that law—first, as a matter of simple equity: American workers should not be paying for the destruction of their own livelihoods.

Second, I will invest the savings from reform in new incentives to create new, good paying jobs here—and to lower corporate taxes by 5% to make all our companies more competitive. Let me be clear: under my plan, 99 percent of American businesses and 98 percent of Americans will get a tax cut.

In coming weeks, I will focus on the health care costs that today burden American enterprise and—for example—make it $1700 more expensive to produce the same car here than it costs in Canada. And I will discuss how America, by investing in new technology, in broadband, and in the great imperative of energy independence can lead the world in the jobs of the future.

Today, I turn to an issue that is essential to all the others because it is the foundation of confidence in our economic future. In the last three years, the federal budget has gone from record surpluses to record deficits—which, if left unchecked, can become a fiscal cancer that will erode any recovery and threaten the prospect of a lasting prosperity. Ultimately, as deficits drive up long term interest rates, they will dry up investment and undermine the belief, at home and overseas, that America is worth investing in.

George Bush now promises to reduce the deficit—the same promise of fiscal responsibility he has made and broken in every year, every budget, and every State of the Union message. The record is clear: a deficit reduction promise from George W. Bush is not exactly a gilt edged bond; and if he continued in the Presidency and performed as he has in the past, a third Bush term could mean a third Bush recession.

When it comes to the federal budget, I will move America in a new direction—by cutting the deficit in half in four years while making health care affordable; by paying for every program I propose; and by rolling back the Bush tax cut for the wealthiest Americans while expanding tax cuts for the middle class.

This will not be easy. It will require tough decisions—not just for one budget or one campaign, but for years to come and often in the face of unforeseen circumstances. But I know we can take this course and stay this course—because we've done it before.

And that is why Americans can trust what I am saying: I have a voting record that, on the most critical budget votes of the last 20 years, helped balance our budget and pay down our debt.

When I first came to the Senate in 1985, the federal deficit was soaring as it is today.

In the 1980's, the national debt clock in New York City became a symbol for a federal deficit and debt that were out-of-control. Back then, many Democrats thought we could spend and spend without having to pay the bill. And back then, most Republicans even claimed that if you gave huge tax cuts to the wealthy, they would somehow pay for themselves. I guess that's what they mean by "an elephant never forgets."

At that the time, I joined together with a group of reformers from both parties—like Republican Senator Warren Rudman and Democratic Senator Fritz Hollings—to push for a deficit reduction plan with real teeth. What we got was real grief from leaders in both parties—and by the early 90s, the deficit was increasing so fast that the debt clock would sometimes breakdown because it couldn't keep up.

We made tough choices in 1993—when a new president challenged the Congress to return to fiscal sanity. And the choice really was tough; fiscal sanity won by exactly one vote. I was proud to cast a deciding vote in the Senate to bring the deficit under control. In 1997, we finished the job by passing an historic bipartisan balanced budget agreement—which not only balanced the budget for the first time since 1969, but extended the life of Medicare, expanded health care for children, and cut taxes for middle-class Americans.

By 2000, we were on the road to saving Social Security and we were paying down our national debt for the first time since Andrew Jackson was president—170 years ago. The numbers on the national debt clock were spinning backwards.

Just before George Bush took office, the clock was taken down. Talk about wishful thinking.

The new president, who had promised to change the partisan tone in Washington, promptly turned his back on the bipartisan balanced budget consensus of the 1990s. Instead of short term decisions to stimulate the economy, he made long term mistakes that exploded the deficit.

He lavished tax cuts we couldn't afford on those who didn't need them. He made a clear choice: to pass the bucks to the privileged while passing the buck to our children. Because of this president's decisions, a child born today will inherit a $20,000 debt—a "Birth Tax" that he or she had no part in creating.

In New York, the national debt clock has been turned back on—with the numbers rising faster than the human eye can see.

In a blink of history's eye, trillions in budget surpluses have been transformed into trillions in deficits over the next decade. From missions to Mars to tax cuts for the wealthy to a Medicare bill that benefits drug companies and burdens seniors, the Bush administration has failed to pay for what it has proposed. This president has proposed or passed $6 trillion in initiatives in the next ten years alone that he has no plan to pay for.

His record shows that we can't trust what he says. And no matter what he says now, the Bush policies will not reduce the deficit but worsen it.

Instead of facing that reality, George Bush stubbornly refuses to change course. When false promises don't work, he tries excuses. Blaming everyone from Bill Clinton to Ken Lay to Saddam Hussein.

But that is not the reason for our own budget crisis. The independent, non-partisan Congressional Budget Office reported last month that 94 percent of the $500 billion deficit for next year is due to George Bush's excessive spending and ineffective tax giveaways for the wealthiest Americans. In fact, his tax cuts alone account for most of the long-term deficit increase.

And the price is being paid in many ways.

This administration has squandered the historic opportunity to use the surpluses to save Social Security. Job creation is slowed by increased uncertainty about our economic future. And we are weakened abroad as well as at home. With our national debt increasingly owned by foreign governments, we devalue our own bargaining power with countries like China when they manipulate their currency to inflate their exports, depress ours, and in effect destroy American jobs.

So the deficit is not just about the numbers and statistics—although they are a damning indictment of the Bush record. The issue of fiscal responsibility will shape our entire economic future. My pledge is to restore fiscal discipline—and my budget plan is built on three economic principles.

First, we will not raise taxes on middle-class Americans; we will lower them.

The Bush administration has engineered the greatest tax shift in American history. Middle-class Americans are now paying more of the national budget; wealthy Americans are paying less. Our present national leadership has transferred the tax burden from wealth to work. We will restore tax fairness. We will expand middle-class tax cuts for families with children and married couples and pass new tax cuts to make education and health care more affordable while cutting our deficit in half.

But for Americans making more than $200,000, we will simply roll back the Bush tax rates to the level they were under Bill Clinton to pay for education and health care. With these resources, we can expand health care for all of our children and cover virtually all Americans while lowering the health care premiums that are squeezing families and hurting job creation.

I realize that honorable people can disagree about whether it makes sense to repeal the recent tax cuts for Americans making more than $200,000 so we can afford to invest in health care and education. I am willing to debate that disagreement at any time or place. It is a fundamental choice about our future and a central choice in this election.

But rather than debating real differences, the Bush campaign is engaged in the politics of deceit and distortion.

They are spending millions of dollars trying to mislead Americans about the basic facts: If you make less than $200,000, you'll get a tax cut under my plan. If you make more than $200,000 a year, you will go back to paying the same tax rates you did with President Clinton and our country will get health care and education. The top 2% will pay more than they do now. Everyone else will get a tax cut under a Kerry administration.

Let me repeat: 98% of individuals—and 99% of companies and small businesses—will pay lower taxes under my plan.

Second, we will impose spending restraints so no one can propose or pass a new program without a way to pay for it. And we'll enforce budget discipline with spending caps. During the 1990s, we had spending caps. We cut the deficit in half and then balanced the budget. And along the way, we created 23 million new jobs, increased family income across the board, and gave middle-class families a tax cut. Because we limited the growth of the government's budget, family budgets were able to grow.

So my budget plan pays for my proposals. In contrast to George Bush's $6 trillion in unpaid-for spending, my plan returns to a concept known as 'pay-as-you-go.'

And in the months ahead, as I put forward new ideas for a stronger, better, more prosperous America, I will state, in specific terms, how to finance them without raising the deficit or middle-class taxes.

I have already shown how we can pay for my health care plan and education. But we can and will do more by reducing or eliminating government programs that don't work.

For example, we'll freeze the federal travel budget, reduce oil royalty exemptions for drilling on federal lands, and cut 100,000 contractors now employed by the federal government. We'll streamline government agencies and commissions and reduce out-of-control administrative costs by five percent. And when we're done, the federal government will be smaller but smarter, more effective and less expensive.

The strong spending caps in my plan will insure that spending doesn't grow faster than inflation. If Congress fails to keep spending in line, the budget caps will mean across the board cuts in every area except security and education and mandatory spending programs like health care, Social Security and Medicare.

So when I say a cap on spending, I mean it. We will have to make real choices—and that includes priorities of my own.

Let me give you a couple of examples. I've proposed a major expansion of national service programs to strengthen the values of patriotism, community and citizenship. And I believe we need to make preschool universal so that every child in America gets the best possible start in life. But with the deficit worsening each and every day of the Bush administration, we may have to slow both initiatives down or phase them in over a longer period. I don't like that. But those are the hard calls a president has to make.

Third, we will free resources and reduce the deficit by taking on corporate welfare. John McCain and I have introduced legislation to end corporate welfare as we know it. In a Kerry administration, we will fight for that bill; we will take our case to the public if we have to—and we will pass it. Today, mining companies buy up public lands for five dollars an acre.

And Dick Cheney's old company Halliburton dodges taxes with offshore havens while it gets billions from no-bid government contracts. If I'm elected president, those days will come to an end.

By going after corporate welfare, as John McCain says, we can save tens of billions of dollars a year. Our bill calls for a Corporate Subsidy Reform Commission to recommend cuts and submit them to Congress for an up or down vote—with no amendments.

John McCain can't get anyone in the Bush White House to listen to our proposal. If I'm president, John McCain will get the first pen when I sign this bill into law.

We can't restore fiscal responsibility unless we have a president willing to bring our divided parties together—and ready to be straight with the public about what we can and can't afford.

We can cut the deficit in half in four years, expand health care coverage, and make it more affordable for the families who already have it. We can invest in education, restore pay as you go rules, and impose spending caps. We can rollback the Bush tax cuts for those at the top—and cut taxes for middle-class Americans.

We can do all this if we set clear national priorities—and make the tough decisions—not just about the programs of others, but about our own proposals.

And we have to do this—because it is critical to any credible economic plan and the creation of new, good-paying jobs. An America that ignores the deficit will be an America that invites inflation and recession.

An America that pays for new initiatives and follows real budget rules will be able to build a new era of prosperity.

We know how to do this. We did it in the 1990s. Now it's time to return our government to fiscal responsibility—and our country to investment in the future, to job creation and rising standards of living.

And if I am president, that is the new direction I will set for our budget and our economy.

None of these choices are about numbers or dollars alone. They are the choices we make that build the fiber of our nation. They are the responsibility our generation has been handed and the legacy that we hand to the generations to come. This is the course we must choose. This is the course we will chart together.

Thank you.

★

"Protecting Our Environment for Future Generations"
Remarks by Senator John Kerry on Earth Day 2004

Thank you. I'm glad to be in Houston on Earth Day.

I've been spending the last few days talking with Americans about how we can build a cleaner, healthier environment. And while there's plenty that we're going to do differently than this Administration on this issue, let me start by saying something nice about President Bush—he is an expert on recycling. He's recycled the same bad Republican policies from the 1980's all over again in the year 2004.

Thank you Dr. Lauren. Your story reminds all of us about a basic American idea: "we can all make a difference and each one of us should try." When it comes to protecting our environment, strengthening our economy, and improving public health, effort is everything.

Whether it's saving our great public spaces like this one, stopping polluters from sending toxins into the water your drink, or protecting those national treasures we count on for our jobs, our livelihoods, and to feed our souls, our responsibility as Americans is to protect and preserve God's gift to human kind.

We only have one chance with this place, and you and I together are going to make sure we use it wisely. We're going to ensure that our values and our beliefs reflect in how we treat our oceans, how we develop our small towns in the mountains, and how we protect our national parks and treasures.

For we are all stewards of our land and water. We are all capable of creating lasting change. And we are all determined to ensure that those Americans who have yet to grace this earth can live in a country that keeps them healthy and gives them the opportunity to reach their full potential.

But you and I know that we cannot succeed unless we change course. We cannot build a stronger America together—an America that protects our air and our water and our children—unless we change course in November.

One of the great traditions in America is an unspoken vow between the old and the young. For generations, older Americans have worked hard to ensure that the America they leave behind is smarter, stronger, and more secure than when they found it.

Yet, for the first time in our history, this tradition may end and an older generation may pass on an America that is in worse shape than when they found it. We're facing trillions of dollars in debt. Our foreign policy has pushed the world aside and left us to face threats on our own. We have a health care crisis that is emptying the pockets of working families. And in three short years, one man and one Administration has put the breaks on 30 years of environmental progress.

Houston, do you want four more years of rolling back our clean air laws that pollute our air and give our kids asthma? Do you want four more years of arsenic in our drinking water? Do you want four more years of mercury levels rising in women and children? Do you want four more years of polluters getting a tax break while you're stuck with the bill? Do you want four more years of ignoring our allies to stop global warming? Neither do I! Their kind of environment is hazardous to our health, our kid's health, and the world's.

We can do better because we know that the environment is about something bigger than a photo-op event once a year. It's about protecting our economy, our public health, and our way of life. They are all connected and they are all endangered if we don't change course in November.

So Houston will you help me change course in November? Will you help me lead America to a place where no soldier ever has to be sent overseas because of our dependence on Mideast oil? Will you help me protect our coastlines and preserve those towns we count on for jobs and to raise our families? Will you help me protect our clean air and clean water laws so that our kids grow up healthy?

Houston will you help me make sure that next Earth Day George Bush celebrates it back home in Texas?

This week I have spent time in Florida and along the coast of Louisiana. I talked about the common sense steps we can take today that will protect those places we love while creating jobs and protecting our economy. This Administration uses the same tired old argument that you can't have a clean environment if you want a strong economy. Well they're wrong. We can have both.

I have a plan that will make this country independent from Mideast oil in ten years. And it will create 500,000 new jobs doing something that's right for our environment, right for our economy, and right to strengthen our national security. We will put that tired old Republican argument to rest when we elect a new president in November!

I have a plan that will protect our oceans and our water ways. I will enforce the BEACHES ACT and provide states with funding so that we know our beachwater is clean. I will work with local officials like Houston's great Mayor Bill White to create strong partnerships to reduce storm-water runoff. I will provide our states and local communities with the resources they need to protect important coastal ecosystems and implement smart coastal development.

And when it comes to mercury, I will not let the utilities off the hook. It just makes sense when 4.9 million women of childbearing age have high levels of mercury, and when one in six new-born infants have levels of mercury so high that they can cause brain damage. You stop the polluters to protect the health of women and children!

Yesterday, I talked about my plan to protect our coastlines. In Louisiana, every 30 minutes a piece of land the size of a football field sinks into the Gulf of

Mexico. Costal erosion isn't just swallowing their beaches; it's drowning their economy. Fishermen see their nets come up empty. Sportsmen watch entire habitats disappear. And families who live and visit those coastline towns fear that their homes or businesses may literally slip away.

We can change this. We can enact laws that conserve and protect coastal regions here and all over America. We will make the protection of our coastlines a national priority, because a secure coastline means security for the families who live there, the business owners who make a living there, and the sportsmen who hunt and fish there.

This is what we can do when we change course in November. All it takes is a president who understands that there are no false choices to make between a clean environment and a strong economy—we can and we will have both when I am president.

We have great local leaders like Mayor Bill White, who are dedicated to making their cities and neighborhoods healthy places to live, work, and raise their families.

Mayor White has been a leader in advocating the use of new technologies to reduce the energy use in buildings. The use of tree planting, paving and roofing materials which reflect, not absorb heat. This could reduce energy bills and over time reduce outside air temperatures. We need to support innovative thinking like that.

You know when I was young I learned this invaluable lesson about our environment from my mother. She taught me how to recycle before it became second nature for so many Americans today. And often, she would wake me up in the middle of the night, take me outside and say, "Listen."

30 years ago, a generation listened to Rachel Carson and her wisdom. I was proud to be apart of that movement then—painted Storrow Drive in Boston a biodegradable green— and throughout my time in the senate.

We saw our country transform from a place where lakes caught fire, there was lead in our gasoline, and polluters had free reign to send anything into our sky, our land, and our water ways. But we put an end to that and we are not going to let this Administration put an end to 30 years of progress.

Thirty-five years ago, when I was on a boat, drifting along Vietnam's Mekong Delta, I grew up with a band of brothers from all walks of life and every corner of America. We learned many things on that journey, but above all, we learned that we were never the kid from South Carolina, Iowa, Arkansas, California, or the kid from Massachusetts.

Under the heat of fire and the fog of battle, our mission became crystal clear, and color, religion, and background melted away. We understood that we were all simply "Americans." All of us fighting under the same flag, praying to the same God.

I'm running for president because I believe that we are all in the same boat, not all on our own. I believe that no matter what our differences, Americans all over this country want pretty much the same things in life. We want to be united, not divided. We want to believe there is more we can do about the problems facing America, not less. We want the opportunity to build a better life, not more barriers to prosperity.

So let's go out of here determined to keep that tradition begun by our forefathers of caring for this great land of ours and handing it on to our children in better shape then we were given it. Let's work our hearts to make sure that the America we pass on is a country with clean rivers, clean air, clean water, with a safer environment that once again sees the smoke from the smokestacks disappear right along with our kid's asthma.

With the right leadership again, we can be a nation that is once again filled with people who never forget that we are not the inheritors of the earth, but the stewards for the future. And when I am president, we will respect that deep rooted value in the United States of America, not just on Earth Day, but every day!

WASHINGTON, D.C.

April 23, 2004

★

Excerpts from

"A Contract with America's Middle Class"
Remarks of Senator John Kerry
at the American Society of Newspaper Editors Convention

...Today, I am introducing my "Contract with America's Middle Class."

The first responsibility of the president is to keep our country safe and secure. And I will. I'm running because we are in a new kind of war, and we need a commander in chief with a plan to fight this war and win it.

Americans have never failed the cause of human freedom, and we will not fail it now—not in Iraq, not in Afghanistan, not anywhere. I have many differences with President Bush over how we should wage the war against terrorism and extremism. I think he made a huge mistake in relying on local Afghan forces to capture Osama bin Laden, rather than committing sufficient U.S. forces on the ground to do the job.

But we share the same goal of total victory. You can count on this: No matter who wins this presidential election, the terrorists will lose.

As president, I will never hesitate to use American power to defend our interests anywhere in the world. I will stand up for our country, our flag and our values, and make it clear that the first definition of patriotism is keeping faith with those who wore the uniform of our country.

I will make America's armed forces even stronger by adding troops so our forces are not spread too thin around the globe and by making sure our forces have the armor and support they need. But what this administration doesn't understand is that to win this war, we must make the world respect America's other sources of strength: our economic engine, our ideals, and our profound purpose to be the last, best hope of earth.

The second priority in my contract with the middle class is this: I will put the economy and government back in line with our values.

The middle class is the moral and economic backbone of this nation. Franklin Roosevelt realized that and he set in motion programs that helped people go to college, buy a house, and build their wealth. The country prospered: we created nearly 11 million new jobs and homeownership increased by 13 percent from 1950-1960.

President Clinton saw the same thing. His plans invested in people and we created 23 million new jobs, 7 million Americans were lifted out of poverty, and more Americans went to college. The middle class built this country. They work hard, pay their bills, and do right by their families and their country. This country ought to do right by them.

For too long, this administration hasn't honored those values, and it certainly hasn't lived up to them. They've put wealth ahead of work, something-for-nothing ahead of responsibility, and special privilege for the few ahead of what's right for the nation.

My plan will create 10 million jobs with a proven strategy built on a simple principle: We should reward work, make sure Americans have a chance to work, and get ahead when they do.

...Third, I will say to America's middle class, and all who wish to join its ranks: I have a plan to raise your income and a commitment to cut your taxes.

On this president's watch, Americans are working harder, earning less, and paying more for health care and college and taxes.

...Meanwhile, the Bush administration has engineered the greatest tax shift in American history. Middle-class Americans are now paying more of the national budget; wealthy Americans are paying less. The middle-class burden has gone up, while incomes have gone down. That's why to build a strong economy, I'll cut middle-class taxes, so middle-class incomes go up.

Throughout this campaign, I have disagreed with those in my own party who would take away the middle-class tax cuts many of us fought for. My economic plan cuts middle-class taxes by three times as much as George Bush. My plan makes it easier for millions of families to pay for health care, and gives families a tax credit on up to $4,000 in college tuition.

...Fourth, I will keep faith with America's middle class by ushering in a new era of reform. I've been a reformer throughout my career. But I know that the job of a reformer is never done. Since I came to the Senate, I've been fighting for reform on every front. I crossed party lines to support Gramm-Rudman-Hollings budget reform in 1985, when fiscal discipline was a dirty word in my own party.

I took what I had learned as a prosecutor, and fought to pass the 100,000 cops program. We changed the way we fight crime in America – and helped cut violent crime by a third.

When my party was divided over welfare, I voted to pass a landmark welfare reform law with tough work requirements and time limits. We cut the welfare rolls in half, cut poverty in single-parent households by a third, and made welfare a second chance, not a way of life.

...On all the issues I've talked about today, the country faces the choice of whether we want to go forward toward strength, or defend the status quo. But to move America forward, no president, and no government can shoulder this burden alone. We cannot be a stronger nation unless the American people do their part. I will never forget the words of the man who inspired me to public life. John Kennedy gave America a set of challenges, not promises, and said what he offered us mattered less than what he would ask of us.

...This is the time for all of us to summon that American spirit to build a stronger country. And I know that the American people are ready. That is why I am running for president. The American people are just waiting to hear their country's call. And when they report to do their part, what a glorious morning for America it will be. Thank you.

★

"50th Anniversary of Brown v. Board of Education: Let America be America Again"

Remarks of Senator John Kerry at the Kansas State Capitol

Thank you for that generous introduction. And thank you for the invitation to join you in honoring the legacy and renewing the hopes of a Supreme Court decision that forever changed our country and our lives. On May 17, 1954, the Supreme Court of the United States declared that separate would never be equal, setting forth a vision of equality that continues to inspire freedom lovers and freedom movements here in America and around the globe. And it started here in Topeka.

But that is no surprise. Topeka has always been a place for making history. Two hundred years ago, Lewis and Clark mapped the site of this city in their journey across the continent. A hundred and fifty years ago, Topeka became the free-state capital battling against pro-slavery LeCompton. And fifty years ago this very day, the next great battle for freedom was centered here in Topeka's segregated schools.

Brown summoned our country to make real the ideal of one nation and one people. A nation where one day all of God's children would live in the light of equality. A nation where, as Dr. King said later, we would be able to "transform ... into a beautiful symphony of brotherhood." Those of us who have embraced this vision redeemed the promise of America and make our country stronger.

It's hard to believe it's been fifty years since Brown. Fifty years since the color of your skin determined where you could get a drink of water. Where you could sit on the bus. Whether you had a seat at the lunch counter. And where you could go to school.

In 1954, in Topeka, there were 18 neighborhood schools for white children and just four "black only" elementary schools. Oliver Brown thought it was wrong that his seven-year-old daughter, Linda and her friends had to walk a mile through a railroad yard every day just to catch a bus to their segregated elementary school. The trip took more than an hour, and on the way, Linda walked right past the closed doors of a white elementary school just 3 blocks from her house. It was separate—but it was not equal. The Supreme Court agreed and that decision became a turning point in America's long march toward equality.

Although the journey here isn't finished, Topeka, has been transformed these fifty years. We are joined here today by Topeka's first African American Mayor, James McClinton. And isn't it a measure of the progress we've made that Topeka has a school superintendent who 50 years ago couldn't have walked the halls of many schools in this city? Today, Tony Sawyer is not only walking the halls, he is commanding the corridors of power of the Topeka school system.

All of America is a better place because of Brown. Back then, only four percent of African Americans had college degrees. Today, nearly twenty percent are college graduates. But we have more to do.

In the 1950s, there were less than 200 black elected officials in all of America, and even fewer Hispanic Americans. Now there are more than 14,000—including the 59 members of the Congressional Black Caucus and the Hispanic Caucus. But we have more to do.

There were no African Americans on the big corporate boards back then. Today, more than forty percent of the Fortune 1000 companies have black directors, and nearly fifteen percent have Latino directors. But we have more to do.

And while it wasn't until six years before Brown that President Truman integrated our military, I can tell you from first-hand experience that service to our country—loyalty to mission and to brother and sister soldiers on the battlefield—knows no color line. Whether we hail from the foothills of Appalachia ... the street corners of Topeka ... the neighborhoods of Flushing ... the barrios of East LA or the reservations of Arizona ... whether we are new immigrants or our descendants came here on the Mayflower or were brought here on a slave ship in shackles ... when we fight side by side in places like Vietnam and Iraq and Afghanistan, we're all

Americans sacrificing for the same country and praying to the same God.

Today, more than ever, we need to renew our commitment to one America. We should not delude ourselves into thinking that the work of Brown is done when there are those who still seek, in different ways, to see it undone. To rollback affirmative action—to restrict equal rights—to undermine the promise of our Constitution.

Yes, we have to defend the progress that has been made. But we also have to move the cause forward. Brown began to tear down the walls of inequality. The next great challenge is to put up a ladder of opportunity for all.

Because as far as we've come, we still have not met the promise of Brown.

We have not met the promise of Brown when one-third of all African American children are living in poverty.

We have not met the promise of Brown when only fifty percent of African American men in New York City have a job.

We have not met the promise of Brown when nearly twenty million black and Hispanic Americans don't have basic health insurance.

And we certainly have not met the promise of Brown when, in too many parts of our country, our school systems are not separate but equal—but they are separate and unequal.

We haven't met the promise of Brown when a fourth grade Hispanic child is only one third as likely to read at the same level as a fourth grade white child. When only fifty percent of African Americans are finishing high school, and only 18 percent are graduating college. Our children will never have equal opportunity unless, once and for all, we close the ever-widening achievement gap. We know the answer is both higher expectations and greater resources. You cannot promise no child left behind and then pursue policies that leave millions of children behind. Because that promise is a promissory note to all of America's families that must be paid in full.

We cannot be content to see nearly four million students in this nation going to schools that are literally crumbling around them. We cannot be content to see those who teach the next generation treated like second-rate employees—not like the professionals they are. We all know from our own lives that good teachers can make all the difference. Yet, today, where the best teachers are needed the most, they're too often paid the least.

So how do we honor the legacy of Brown? That question was answered some 20 years before that decision by a son of Lawrence, Kansas and one of America's greatest poets—Langston Hughes. In one of his most soul wrenching poems, Hughes challenged the nation to "Let America Be America Again." He called that generation to fulfill the unmet promise of America:

> O' let my land be a land where liberty
> Is crowned with no false patriotic wreath
> But opportunity is real, and life is free,
> Equality is in the air we breathe.

And so we honor the legacy of Brown by letting America be America—by reaffirming the value of inclusion, equality, and diversity in our schools and across the life of our nation. By opening the doors of opportunity, so that more of our young people can stay in school and out of prison. By lifting more of our people out of poverty, expanding the middle class, providing health care, and bringing jobs, hope and opportunity to all the neighborhoods of the forgotten America.

We must let America be America again. We must work together to turn back the creeping tide of division that Thurgood Marshall and so many others fought so hard against.

We must never forget that the Brown decision came in the wake of World War II, when African-American soldiers helped to save freedom in the world, only to return to brutal inequality at home. They did not ask for special treatment or extra help; they just wanted the fullness of freedom in their own lives. They wanted to see the end of the "white only" signs at the restaurants and movie theaters, at school house doors and department stores—and they wanted to see an end to the invisible, but all too real "white only" sign that reached from Congress into every great corporation and into businesses in small towns.

And when I joined so many other veterans of Vietnam for a return without welcome to America I saw first hand how those on the front lines of combat, black and brown, who had been casualties in greater numbers than the representation of our population, were shunned even after service. Their unemployment numbers were higher. Their opportunities were less than those with whom they had served and the ravages of post-war trauma fell even more heavily on their families and their lives.

The memory of all of these patriots and the decision we commemorate today calls us again to the America we must become. Our brave men and women who are on frontlines far away deserve no less. For them and for our country, fifty years after Brown we have only just begun. For America to be America for any of us, America must be America for all of us.

Thank you and God bless you.

★

"Security and Strength for a New World"
Remarks of Senator John Kerry at Pier 62

Thank you all for being here.

Over the next ten days, our nation will come together to honor the bravery and sacrifice of past generations of Americans. On Saturday, in our nation's capital, we will dedicate a memorial to the heroes of the Greatest Generation who won World War II. On Memorial Day, we will salute all those who for more than two centuries made the ultimate sacrifice when America's freedom was on the line.

And on June 6th, we will mark the 60th anniversary of D-Day by remembering the brave young men who scaled the cliffs on beaches called Omaha and Utah— and brought the light of liberty from the New World to the Old.

To me, and to millions of Americans, the days ahead will be filled with the pride of families, the sadness of loss and a renewed commitment to service. But that is not enough. We must pay tribute.

We must hear and heed the lessons of the Greatest Generation.

Our leaders then understood that America drew its power not only from the might of weapons, but also from the trust and respect of nations around the globe. There was a time, not so long ago, when the might of our alliances was a driving force in the survival and success of freedom—in two World Wars, in the long years of the Cold War—then from the Gulf War to Bosnia and Kosovo. America led instead of going it alone. We extended a hand, not a fist. We respected the world—and the world respected us.

More than a century ago, Teddy Roosevelt defined American leadership in foreign policy. He said America should walk softly and carry a big stick. Time and again, this administration has violated the fundamental tenet of Roosevelt's approach, as he described it: "If a man continually blusters, if he lacks civility, a big stick will not save him from trouble."

But that is precisely what this administration has done. They looked to force before exhausting diplomacy. They bullied when they should have persuaded.

They have gone it alone when they should have assembled a team. They have hoped for the best when they should have prepared for the worst. In short, they have undermined the legacy of generations of American leadership. And that is what we must restore.

Today, there is still a powerful yearning around the world for an America that listens and leads again. An America that is respected, and not just feared.

I believe that respect is an indispensable mark of our nation's character—and an indispensable source of our nation's strength. It is the indispensable bond of America's mighty alliances.

I'm running for president because, abroad as well as at home, it's time to let America be America again. By doing so, we can restore our place in the world and make America safer.

It's time for a new national security policy guided by four new imperatives: First, we must launch and lead a new era of alliances for the post 9-11 world. Second, we must modernize the world's most powerful military to meet the new threats. Third, in addition to our military might, we must deploy all that is in America's arsenal—our diplomacy, our intelligence system, our economic power, and the appeal of our values and ideas. Fourth and finally, to secure our full independence and freedom, we must free America from its dangerous dependence on Mideast oil.

These four imperatives are a response to an inescapable reality: War has changed; the enemy is different—and we must think and act anew.

Today, we are waging a global war against a terrorist movement committed to our destruction. Terrorists like al Qaeda and its copycat killers are unlike any adversary our nation has faced. We do not know for certain how they are organized or how many operatives they have. But we know the destruction they can inflict.

We saw it in New York and in Washington; we have seen it in Bali and in Madrid, in Israel and across the Middle East; and we see it day after day in Iraq.

This threat will only be magnified as the technology to build nuclear and biological weapons continues to spread. And we can only imagine what would happen if the deadly forces of terrorism got their hands on the deadliest weapons in history.

Everyone outside the administration seems to understand that we are in deep trouble in Iraq. Failure there would be a terrible setback. It would be a boon to our enemies, and jeopardize the long-term prospects for a peaceful, democratic Middle East—leaving us at war not just with a small, radical minority, but with increasingly large portions of the entire Muslim world.

There is also the continuing instability in Afghanistan, where al Qaeda still has a base, and Osama bin Laden is still at large, because the Bush administration didn't finish him off at the battle of Tora Bora. And in East Asia, North Korea poses a genuine nuclear threat, while we have begun to strip American troops to relieve the overburdened forces in Iraq.

In the coming week, I will also offer specific plans to build a new military capable of defeating enemies new and old, and to stop the spread of nuclear, biological and chemical weapons. But first, here today, I want to set out the overall architecture of a new policy to make America stronger and respected in the world.

The first new imperative represents a return to the principle that guided us in peril and victory through the past century—alliances matter, and the United States must lead them.

Never has this been more true than in the war on terrorism.

As president, my number one security goal will be to prevent the terrorists from gaining weapons of mass murder. And our overriding mission will be to disrupt and destroy their terrorist cells.

Because al Qaeda is a network with many branches, we must take the fight to the enemy on every continent—and enlist other countries in that cause.

America must always be the world's paramount military power. But we can magnify our power through alliances. We simply can't go it alone—or rely on a coalition of the few. The threat of terrorism demands alliances on a global scale—to find the extremist groups, to guard ports and stadiums, to share intelligence, and to get the terrorists before they get us. In short, we need a "coalition of the able"—and in truth, no force on earth is more able than the United States and its allies.

We must build that force—and we can. We can be strong without being stubborn. Indeed, that is ultimately the only way we can succeed.

Building strong alliances is only the first step. We cannot meet the new threats unless our military is adapted for new missions. This is my second new imperative.

As president, on my first day in office, I will send a message to every man and woman in our armed forces: This commander-in-chief will ensure that you are the best-led, best-equipped and most respected fighting force in the world. You will be armed with the right weapons, schooled in the right skills, and fully prepared to win on the battlefield. But you will never be sent into harm's way without enough troops for the task, or asked to fight a war without a plan to win the peace.

And you will never be given assignments which have not been clearly defined and for which you are not professionally trained.

This administration has disregarded the advice, wisdom, and experience of our professional military officers. And often ended the careers of those who dared to give their honest assessments. That is not the way to make the most solemn decisions of war and peace. As president, I will listen to and respect the views of our experienced military leaders—and never let ideology trump the truth.

In the past, when our leaders envisioned the use of force, they had in mind the unleashing of massive numbers of American troops, battleships and aircraft in confrontation with the uniformed military of an enemy nation. Of course, a conventional war to halt conventional aggression still remains a possibility for which we must prepare. But there are other urgent challenges.

I will modernize our military to match its new missions. We must get the most out of new technologies. We must reform training and update the way we structure our armed forces—for example, with Special Forces designed to strike terrorists in their sanctuaries, and with National Guard and Reserve units retooled to meet the requirements of homeland defense.

This strategy focuses not only on what we must do, but on what we must prevent. We must ensure that lawless states and terrorists will not be armed with weapons of mass destruction.

This is the single gravest threat to our security. Any potential adversary should know that we will defend ourselves against the possibility of attack by unconventional arms. If such a strike does occur, as commander-in-chief, I will respond with overwhelming and devastating force. If such an attack appears imminent, as commander-in-chief, I will do whatever is necessary to stop it. And, as commander-in-chief, I will never cede our security to anyone. I will always do what is necessary to safeguard our country.

The Justice Department said yesterday that terrorists may be planning to attack the United States again this summer—some believe that al Qaeda would use an attack to try and influence the outcome of the November election.

I have a message today for al Qaeda or any terrorist who may be harboring these illusions: We may have an election here in America. But let there be no doubt—this country is united in its determination to destroy you. And let me be absolutely clear: As commander-in-chief, I will bring the full force of our nation's power to bear on finding and crushing your networks. We will use every available resource to destroy you.

But not all problems should be viewed through a military lens. We should never wait to act until we have no other choice but war. That brings me to my third new imperative.

In this new world, beyond military power, we must deploy all the power in America's arsenal.

We need to employ a layered defense to keep the worst weapons from falling into the worst hands. A strategy that invokes our non-military strength early enough and effectively enough so military force doesn't become our only option.

As president, I will launch a global initiative to fully secure the materials needed for nuclear weapons that already exist and sharply limit and control future production.

This initiative will include changes in international treaties, sharing of intelligence, and setting conditions for economic sanctions and the interdiction of illegal shipments. The key is for America to lead: to build an international consensus for early preventive action, so that states don't even think of taking the nuclear road, and potential traffickers in nuclear and biological technology fear the consequences of getting caught.

We must also have the best possible intelligence capabilities. Nothing is more important than early warning and specific information when dangerous technologies are being developed or sold. Whether it was September 11th or Iraq's supposed weapons of mass destruction, we have endured too many intelligence failures. That is why I will do what this president has failed to do: reform our intelligence system by making the next director of the CIA a true director of national intelligence, with true control over intelligence personnel and budgets all across the government.

All the levers of power will be deployed to overcome the 21st century dangers we face. I intend to discuss this initiative in detail early next week.

Finally, a new national security policy demands an end to our dependence on Mideast oil. That is my fourth new imperative. For too long, America has lost its voice when talking about the policies and practices of some governments in the Persian Gulf.

We have been constrained by their control over the oil that fuels too large a part of our economy. This is a weakness that this administration has ignored—and one that must be addressed.

I have proposed a plan for energy independence from Mideast oil in the next ten years. It invests in new technologies and alternative fuels. It provides tax credits to help consumers buy and manufacturers build fuel efficient cars. It will tap America's initiative and ingenuity to strengthen our national security, grow our economy, and protect our environment.

If we are serious about energy independence, then we can finally be serious about confronting the role of Saudi Arabia in financing and providing ideological support of al Qaeda and other terrorist groups. We cannot continue this administration's kid-glove approach to the supply and laundering of terrorist money. As president, I will impose tough financial sanctions against nations or banks that engage in money laundering or fail to act against it. I will launch a "name and shame" campaign against those that are financing terror. And if they do not respond, they will be shut out of the U.S. financial system.

The same goes for Saudi sponsorship of clerics who promote the ideology of Islamic terror. To put it simply, we will not do business as usual with Saudi Arabia. They must take concrete steps to stop their clerics from fueling the fires of Islamic extremism.

Let me now turn to a subject that I know is on the minds of all Americans—the situation in Iraq.

The stakes in Iraq couldn't be higher. Earlier this week, the president again said he wanted to create stability and establish a representative government in Iraq. He did acknowledge what many have known all along—that we would be far better off if our allies were with us. What's important now is to turn these words into action.

In the coming weeks, President Bush will travel to Europe and meet with the members of the G-8 here in the United States. There will be speeches, handshakes and ceremonies. But will our allies promise to send more troops to Iraq? Will they dedicate substantially more funding for reconstruction there? Will they pledge a real effort to aid the transformation of the Middle East. That is what we need. But the day is late and the situation in Iraq is grim.

Attracting international support in a situation like Iraq is a clear test of presidential leadership. It is what capable and confident presidents do. I urge President Bush to make a sustained effort. He should start at the Summit in Istanbul by persuading NATO to accept Iraq as an alliance mission, with more troops from NATO and its partners. He should seek help in expanding international support for training Iraq's own security forces, so they can safeguard the rights and well-being of their own people.

And he should propose the creation of an International High Commissioner to work with Iraqis in organizing elections, drafting a constitution, and coordinating reconstruction.

Over the last year, we've heard from the president that our policy should simply be to stay the course. But one thing I learned in the Navy is that when the course you're on is headed for the shoals, you have to change course.

If President Bush doesn't secure new support from our allies, we will, once again, feel the consequences of a foreign policy that has divided the world instead of uniting it. Our troops will be in greater peril, the mission in Iraq will be harder to accomplish, and our country will be less secure.

I have spoken today about the architecture of a new national security policy. But at issue here is not just a set of prescriptions; at stake is a vision of an America truly stronger and truly respected in the world. This is not a partisan cause. Patriotism doesn't belong to any one Party or president. And if I am president, I will enlist the best among us, regardless of party, to protect the security of this nation.

And I will call on the whole nation to let America be America again.

My father was a pilot during World War II. A year before Pearl Harbor, he was on active duty and he later served in the South Pacific.

And for the rest of his life, he served in one capacity or another—whether nationally or locally, by vocation or as a volunteer.

He told me shortly before he died that the "human conscience, when it works is the most divine thing in our small segment of the universe."

In today's world, conscience marks the difference between tolerance and terror.

In an earlier era, it was the difference between honor and holocaust.

Much has been written about the Greatest Generation.

The question before us now is what will be said about our own.

Because, for better or worse, as Abraham Lincoln once said, we cannot escape the judgment of history.

We do not have to live in fear or stand alone. We don't have to be a lonely "watchman on the walls of freedom." We can, once again, lead a great alliance. That is how we can honor the legacy of the Greatest Generation and restore respect to the greatest country—the United States of America.

Thank you and God bless America.

★

"Strengthening Our Military"
Remarks of Senator John Kerry
at the Harry S. Truman Library and Museum

Thank you, General Wilson for that kind introduction, and thank you all for coming today. General Wilson is the quintessential example of what we mean by the opportunity Army. He rose from private to Commander of the Army Materiel Command, supplying the Army with everything from beans, to bullets, to boots. And I'm delighted that he's with us today.

I can't tell you what a treat it is for me to stand here this afternoon in this remarkable library celebrating a remarkable man. In word and deed, Harry Truman embodied the highest ideals of the Greatest Generation. He desegregated our armed forces. He created the Marshall Plan that rebuilt Europe from the ground up, and gave life to the United Nations and NATO. And he set this nation and the world on a wise and patient path to win the Cold War without a third World War.

President Truman understood that our military is only as good as the men and women in its ranks. And I know that he would be as proud of the soldiers who serve this country today as he was of those who sacrificed for our country sixty years ago.

In the spirit of all the men and women in uniform we honor at this time every year, let me offer this pledge: As president, I will always remember that America's security begins and ends with the soldier, sailor, airman, and marine—with every man and every woman in our armed services standing a post somewhere in the world. Today, we salute each and every one of them for their commitment, strength, and extraordinary courage—especially those serving in Iraq and Afghanistan. They, like all veterans of wars past, deserve our prayers and then, when they come home, they deserve the respect and support of a grateful nation. After all, the first definition of patriotism is to keep faith with those who have worn the uniform of the United States.

And the first duty of a commander in chief is to make America strong and keep Americans safe. A week ago in Seattle, I outlined a new strategy of national security based on four imperatives. First, we must lead strong alliances for the post 9-11 world. Second, to secure our full independence and freedom, we must free America from its dangerous dependence on Mideast oil. Third, in addition to our military might, we must deploy all that is in America's arsenal—our diplomacy, our intelligence, our economic power, and the power of our values and ideas.

And fourth is the imperative I will discuss today: We must modernize the world's most powerful military to meet new and different threats. The Bush administration was right to call for the "transformation" of the military. But their version of transformation was directed at fighting classic conventional wars, rather than the dangers we now face in Iraq, Afghanistan, and in the war against al Qaeda. To rise to the challenges we face, we must strengthen our military, including our Special Forces; improve our technology; and task our National Guard with Homeland Security.

And there's a reason I decided to come here, to the birthplace of President Truman, to deliver this speech.

In 1945, Franklin Roosevelt died unexpectedly, leaving his vice president of only eighty-three days, Harry S. Truman, to finish a war that had claimed the lives of 400,000 Americans. Beyond the war, the new president inherited a shattered Europe and a divided world, with the warmth of democracy on one side and the chill of communism on the other.

In describing what he saw before him that day, Harry Truman said: "I feel as though the moon and all the stars and all the planets have fallen upon me." In many ways, they had. But that plain spoken son of Missouri rose to a responsibility as grave as any given to any president. In a world divided between freedom and tyranny, his decisions set a course that saved the future of humanity.

To contain communism, and build a mighty alliance, Truman had to rebuild our military both to deter conventional aggression and the threat of nuclear weapons, because, as he put it, "The will for peace without the strength for peace is of no avail." He modernized our armed forces by creating the Department of Defense and the Air Force—the greatest change in our nation's military structure since the beginning of the Republic.

Today, in the post 9-11 world, we stand at another historic crossroad, at another moment when the old enemy is gone but we face a new threat. We must change if we are to meet and defeat the danger. We must reshape our military and prepare it for the risks and tasks of a new era.

Terrorist groups like al Qaeda and its copycat killers are claiming the right to execute the innocent. They confuse murder with martyrdom and fanaticism with faith. They use terror as a sword and religion as a shield.

They present the central national security challenge of our generation. But they are unlike any other adversary our nation has ever confronted. They have no president, capital city, territory, army, or national identity. We are not absolutely certain how they are organized or how many operatives they have. But we know the destruction they can inflict. We saw it here in America on September 11th. We saw it in Bali and in Madrid, and across the Middle East. And now we see it day after day in Iraq. To defeat these threats, we must draw on the four imperatives I described earlier—especially the need to modernize America's military.

Despite all its talk of transforming that military, the Bush administration has done far too little to adapt our forces to the new missions they must undertake.

We went into Iraq with too few troops to prevent looting and crime, and we failed to secure nearly a million tons of conventional weapons now being used against our troops. We failed to build alliances and squandered the opportunity to generate wider support inside Iraq, in the Arab world, and among the major powers. These mistakes have complicated our mission: a stable Iraq with a representative government secure in its borders.

But as hard as it is to believe, there is little evidence that this administration has learned from its mistakes. The rhetoric of toughness is not enough to make us safe. We need tough decisions to strengthen the American military, so we can find and get the terrorists before they get us. As president, I will build a highly-trained military, with more ground troops and Special Forces not just to win war, but to win the peace.

Instead of over-relying on weapons and tactics to fight the battles of the past, against enemies out in the desert or on open seas, we must build mobile and modern forces to prevail against terrorists hiding in caves or in the heart of a city. We must broaden our capabilities to create a military ready for any mission, from armored battle to urban warfare to homeland security. Yes, we must invest in missile defense. But not at the cost of other pressing priorities. We cannot afford to spend billions to deploy an unproven missile defense system. Not only is it not ready, but it's the wrong priority for a war on terror where the enemy strikes with a bomb in the back of a truck, or a vial of anthrax in a briefcase.

This is part of a larger problem. From day one, this administration has been obsessed with threats from other states—instead of opening their eyes to the perils of the new century: terrorist organizations with or without ties to rogue nations and failed states that can become their sanctuaries. These are the enemies our military is facing. And this is where we must train, arm, and equip our military to win.

In addition, we must secure our own democracy and our own borders. Homeland security must be a top priority of the president. Today, it's too often something this administration just pays lip service to when the cameras are rolling.

We can't meet the new threats of this new century with a military from the last one. We must always be ready for strategic and conventional missions. But we must also be committed to build the strongest possible military to meet the new and greatest threats. I'm running for president to build a new military for a new time.

My first order of business as commander in chief will be to expand America's active duty forces. Not to increase the number of soldiers in Iraq, but to add 40,000 new soldiers to prevent and prepare for other possible conflicts. The fact is, the war in Iraq has taken a real toll on our armed services. Nine out of ten active duty Army divisions—ninety percent of the Army's active duty combat divisions—are committed to Iraq, either currently there, preparing to go, or recently returned. That is a dangerous and potentially disastrous course that limits our capacity to respond to other crises.

The war has been especially tough on the Army's critical post-war specialists. Civil affairs. Military police. Combat support units. Psychological operations units. All are in short supply. All are nearly exhausted.

To pick up the slack, since 9-11, we've called up our Guard and Reserves at historic levels. Currently there are more than 165,000 Guardsman and Reservists on active duty. In fact, 40 percent of our forces in Iraq are from the Reserve and the Guard. They are America's workers, doctors, mechanics, and first-responders. Some have been on the ground in Iraq for as many as 15 months—much longer than was expected or promised. And many of these units are being pushed to the limit.

The people of Missouri understand this situation well. More than 800 of your sons and daughters have had their deployments extended and their homecomings delayed. The administration is even planning to send troops from the 11th Armored Cavalry Regiment to Iraq—a unit whose primary mission has been to prepare other units for future deployments.

The effect is clear: our soldiers are stretched too thin.

The administration's answer has been to put band-aids on the problem. They have effectively used a stop-loss policy as a back door draft. They have extended tours of duty, delayed retirements, and prevented enlisted personnel from leaving the service. Just yesterday, the Army announced this would affect even more soldiers whose units are headed to Iraq and Afghanistan. By employing these expedients, they've increased the forces by 30,000 troops.

But this has happened on the backs of the men and women who've already fulfilled their obligation to the armed forces and to our country—and it runs counter to the traditions of an all-volunteer military. Because they're serving one tour after another, our soldiers are not getting the training they need or the rest they deserve. Military families are under incredible strain as it becomes harder and harder to balance the demands of family life and military duty. This is especially true at a time when more than half of our military is married—a dramatic increase since Vietnam. When you add it up, we are in danger of creating another hollow Army—a grave concern that I've heard time and again over the last few months from active duty personnel. I heard it in Pittsburgh from an Army Reserve Captain who had just returned from Iraq. Like me, he fears that our military will not be ready for the next mission. That's not the way to make America safer.

The 40,000 new troops I am adding will not be soldiers who've already been on the front lines, but new volunteers trained and ready to defend their country. And this will help relieve the strain on our troops; it will bring more of our soldiers, guardsmen and reservists back home to their families and get them time for the new training they need.

But numbers alone won't win the war in Iraq or the war on terror. We need to create a "New Total Force." Our military must be prepared to defeat any enemy, anytime, any place. And our soldiers must be capable of success in any conflict.

As president, I will double our Special Forces capability to fight the war on terror. That's the second part of my plan to modernize the military. Our Special Forces are the troops who land behind enemy lines, conduct counter-terrorism operations, perform reconnaissance missions, and gather intelligence. In Afghanistan, after September 11th, they took the fight to the Taliban with remarkable creativity. They also train local forces to take on the responsibilities themselves and they build the relationships that are vital for our victory in the war on terror. We saw what they could do during the Iraq war, when two teams of American Green Berets totaling 31 men worked with Kurdish troops to defeat an Iraqi force numbering in the hundreds. The victory at the battle of Debecka Pass is a tribute to the flexibility, training, and courage of American Special Forces—all essential to winning the war on terror.

We must also recognize that the battle itself is only half the mission. In any conflict, we need an expanded, well-trained force, with soldiers prepared for both war and its aftermath.

As president, I will also increase our civil affairs personnel—those who arrive on the scene after the conflict is over and help win the peace. They work with local leaders and officials to get the schools back in shape, the hospitals reopened, and banks up and running.

We also need—and a Kerry administration will provide—more military police, because public order is a critical step to winning the peace. At the same time, we should move greater responsibility for non-military missions to civilian agencies to ease the burden on our troops.

As president, I will build a modern military, with the best trained troops and the most modern equipment and technology. That's the third part of my plan. The war in

Iraq has left us with a hefty bill to pay. Our equipment is worn from the daily assault of battle and the harsh effects of an unforgiving desert. We must repair, replace, and upgrade it to maintain the highest level of readiness.

We can't have a 21st century military unless we're using 21st century technology and preparing our forces for 21st century threats. We need a military that is equipped for the next fight, not the last one. That means educating, training, and arming every soldier with state-of-the-art equipment, whether it's body armor or weapons. And it means employing the most sophisticated communications to help our troops prevail and protect themselves in battle. Right now, the technology exists to let a soldier see what's over the next hill or around the next bend in the road. Every soldier in every unit should have access to that modern breakthrough, which can be the difference between life and death. As president, I will see to it that they do.

I will also accelerate the development of non-lethal technologies, like directed energy weapons, that can incapacitate the enemy, without risking the lives of innocent bystanders. The need for this technology is driven by pure military strategy. With more of the world's populations living in cities, it's more critical than ever that our military be able to carry out their missions with the least harm to civilians. As we saw in Fallujah and Najaf, our forces may advance on the ground, but innocent casualties can cost us victory in the minds of the people. This is especially true in the war on terror, where our forces must track down leaders and their cells no matter where they're hiding, even if it's in the center of a densely populated city.

Technology also plays a critical role in keeping the worst weapons out of the hands of rogue states and terrorists. On Tuesday, I proposed a broad agenda to limit the spread of nuclear weapons and material. But we must recognize if the worst does happen, and dangerous weapons technology falls into the wrong hands, the president must have at his disposal every instrument of force necessary to destroy those weapons before they are used against the United States, its citizens, or its allies. Before the war in Afghanistan, there were troubling reports that our military lacked forces specifically trained and targeted to seizing and dismantling nuclear, chemical and biological weapons. We simply can't win the war on terror if we can't control the world's most lethal weapons. As president, I will build new forces that specialize in finding, securing, and destroying weapons of mass destruction and the facilities that build them.

However, technology alone isn't the answer. We must educate and train our forces differently. This commitment to innovation must be wedded to a continuing investment in the men and women of the American military. Their training, education, and professional development will transform this new technology into real military power.

But one thing we've all learned in the war on terror is that America can't lead abroad unless we're secure at home. While this administration has taken steps to protect our borders, they've left out a key asset in the fight on terror—our National Guard. The Guard has kept our nation safe since the militias gathered at Lexington and Concord. They've served in every war, and they're serving now. In fact, after September 11th, they were the first ones called on to line city streets, guard bridges, and patrol our airports.

But today, too many of them are far away from home and the Guard as a whole is not integrated into an effective strategy for homeland security. The National Guard was intended to complement, not be a substitute for, active duty forces. Sending thousands of National Guard members to Iraq has actually weakened our ability to defend our own country. Members of the Guard are first responders across the country—fire fighters, police officers, and emergency medical technicians. To take them out of their communities is to take down a critical first line of defense. That's no way to protect America.

As president, I will make homeland security one of the primary missions of the National Guard. While the military can't solve the entire homeland security challenge, the National Guard can make an important contribution to the mission. That's the fourth part of my plan—modernizing our National Guard. I will assign Guard units to a standing joint task force, commanded by a General from the Guard. This task force will prepare and, if necessary, execute a coordinated strategy for homeland safety, working with the states and the federal government to react in times of crisis.

Just as it was in the time of Harry Truman, and in all the years of the Cold War, the job of commander in chief is now central to the presidency. As president, I will use military force to protect our interests anywhere in the world, whenever necessary. But strong leadership demands more than the willingness to use force. It means directing the use of the right tools at the right time for the right purpose and the right cause. Only then will we be strong and respected around the world.

Strong leadership means striking a balance between the Department of Defense and the other agencies focused on America's national security. It means coordinating our national power rather than competing for bureaucratic power. It means building a first-rate intelligence community, because no president can act wisely without it.

Strong leadership means listening to and respecting the advice, wisdom, and experience of our professional military—and never letting ideology trump the truth. It means working with Congress in a bipartisan fashion to make our military stronger.

Strong leadership means setting goals for a new military, insisting on progress, and seeing the mission through to success.

Strong leadership means building alliances to help win the war on terror and stem the spread of nuclear, biological or chemical weapons.

If Harry Truman were standing here today, I know that he would believe, as I do, that America's strength demands a new military for a new time—what he once called "the strongest, toughest and most enduring forces in the world."

Above all, as president, I will never forget the pledge with which I began today: I will always remember that our security and our strength begins with a single soldier, standing a single post somewhere in the world. And we should be grateful to the men and women willing to do it, with such grace and such courage.

★

"Creating a New Community of the Americas"

Remarks of Senator John Kerry to the National Association
of Latino Elected and Appointed Officials

I want to thank all of you for coming today. It's wonderful to be back at NALEO. Last year, we met in Arizona. This year, we're in Washington. We're clearly headed in the right direction. With your help, next year we'll have a new place to meet just a few blocks from here.

Last summer, when we met, the primaries were just heating up. Since things turned out so well, I've decided that coming here must've been a good idea. So I'm going to keep coming back. Because together we can take back the White House—and put more of you in elected offices all across America.

I want to thank you for the work you're doing every day to build a stronger America. Hispanics may be the fastest growing group in our country, but you've always held on to your basic values—values that built America: strong families, deep faith, and closely-knit communities. You have never forgotten what Cesar Chavez once said, "We cannot seek achievement for ourselves and forget about progress and prosperity for our community." From the boardroom to the barrio, you embody the American ideal—out of many, we are one. And as you have shown us, now, more than ever, we must stand as one America.

Today, thanks to you, we are one step closer to an America that's stronger at home and respected in the world. And that's what I want to talk about this morning: how together we can create opportunity for Hispanics here at home and build stronger relationships with Latin America.

We're here to fight for good-paying jobs that let American workers actually get ahead.

We're here to make health care a right for all of our people.

We're here to make this nation energy independent.

And we're here to build a strong military, and lead strong alliances, so that our military is never overextended and young Americans are never put in harm's way because we went it alone.

You know, I was born in an Army hospital in Denver, Colorado when my father was a pilot in World War II. My father and my mother taught me the value of service.

I've always been determined to give something back to my country—as a soldier, as a prosecutor, as a Senator. And now, I'm running for president. It's been a great adventure and a great privilege. So many of you have welcomed Teresa and me into your homes and hearts. You have told us the stories of your lives—and they have become the work of my life.

The poet Langston Hughes told the stories in this way: "Let America be America again. Let it be the dream it used to be"—for those "whose sweat and blood, whose faith and pain, whose hand at the foundry, whose plow in the rain must bring back our mighty dream again."

In 2004, we have to bring back our mighty dream again. We have to make America all that it can become.

You know, working families all across our country are living by the oldest and greatest of American values—hard work, service, and caring for one another.

And I'm running for president because I believe that our government should live by those values, too.

It's time to remember a basic truth: a stronger America begins right here at home.

In the last three years, Hispanic American unemployment has soared more than 30 percent. 1.4 million Hispanic Americans are out of work. And those finally getting jobs, are being paid an average of $9000 less a year.

But, as you know better than anybody, as wages are going down, Latino health care costs are going up; tuitions are going up; bills are going up. So, more and more Latinos are working weekends; some of them are working two jobs, three jobs—and they're still not getting ahead.

And to add insult to injury, their hard-earned tax dollars are actually paying corporations to export good American jobs.

Twenty years ago, middle-class families with one parent working used to be able to buy a home and pay for college. But today, two incomes barely cover the basics.

And, as you know too well, if anything at all goes wrong—an illness or a temporary layoff—most families can't pay the bills and they risk losing everything they've built and saved for.

In America, a rising tide is supposed to lift all boats. But today, the middle-class boat is taking on water. Like most Americans, I believe we can do better than 1.9 million lost private sector jobs, rising costs, and shrinking incomes. I believe in the American economy and American workers.

We all know that the middle class built this country. Franklin Roosevelt understood that. And so did Bill Clinton. But for nearly four years now, Washington has ignored the middle class, putting wealth ahead of work, something-for-nothing ahead of responsibility, and what's right for the few ahead of what's right for America.

I believe in building up our great middle class—especially the millions of Hispanic Americans coming into the middle class—respecting their work, honoring their values, and lifting them up in the toughest of times. I'm running for president because I want an economy that strengthens and expands the middle class, not one that squeezes it.

We're going to cut taxes for the middle class. And we're going to rollback the Bush tax cuts for those who make over $200,000 a year, invest in education, in health care, and we're going to cut the deficit in half.

I want middle-class taxes to go down, so your incomes go up.

Let me tell you, we need a president who fights for your job as hard as he fights for his own.

I have a plan to put good paying jobs at the heart of our economy. And when I'm president, American taxpayers will never again subsidize the loss of their own jobs.

We're going to close tax loopholes that pay companies to move our jobs overseas—and we're going to reward companies that create good jobs here in America.

My plan calls for tough enforcement of our trade agreements. We're gonna stop other countries from violating those agreements and walking away with the store. Because I'll tell you what I've seen traveling across this country, if you give American workers a fair playing field, there's no one in the world that the American worker can't compete against.

Trade with our neighbors will make us all stronger. But trade without respect is not what our neighbors want—and neither is one-note insistence on free trade agreements. We need to lift up living standards and working conditions for all working men and women in the U.S. and around the world. As president, I will fight for labor and environment protections in every single trade agreement.

I will also work to strengthen our economic and political ties with our neighbors in Latin America, the Caribbean and Canada. I will bring us back to the negotiating table to develop a Central American Free Trade Agreement that provides economic benefits, creates jobs and includes strong protections for labor and the environment. And I will do the same in our negotiations for the Free Trade Area of the Americas.

Let America be America again.

Being strong at home means extending educational opportunity to every child in America, wherever they live, wherever their parents came from. We need to make sure there is a great teacher in every classroom, especially in our hardest pressed communities, and especially for kids who are learning English in our schools. And through programs like GEAR UP and TRIO, we need to reach out to our children and send them a clear message: if you work hard, if you stick with it, not only will you finish high school, but we will make sure you can afford college, graduate, live the American Dream.

And being strong at home means health care that is affordable and accessible to all Americans.

Right now, there are millions of Americans—including one out of every three Latinos—who go to bed every night without basic health care. And I've met scores of them. Families with names like Gutierrez, Garcia, and Martinez.

I'm running for president because I believe their family's health care is just as important as any politician's in Washington, D.C.

Let me just ask you:

Have your health insurance premiums gone up in the last few years?

Have your co-payments gone up?

Have your deductibles gone up?

Then you need to tell this Administration we're fed up and their time is up.

For almost four years, they've had no plan, while rising health care costs are hurting families and making it harder and harder for businesses to compete. My plan will take on the waste and greed in the health care system. It will reduce the average premium by $1,000 a year. It will expand coverage to 95 percent of Americans, including 99 percent of our kids. And, it will crack down on skyrocketing drug prices.

This Administration has it absolutely backwards. They say it's alright to export American jobs. Well, I say it's only right to let Americans import prescription drugs from Canada.

They say we should give billions more to big drug companies. I say we should give seniors a real prescription drug benefit under Medicare.

And in a Kerry Administration, we will stop being the only advanced nation in the world which fails to understand that health care is not a privilege for the elected and the connected or the wealthy—it is a right for every American—so let America be America again.

And being strong at home means always remembering that we are a nation of immigrants. America wouldn't be where it is today—as a country and as a people—if it weren't for immigrants. And neither would I—because I married one! My wife Teresa was raised under a dictatorship in Mozambique. She didn't get to cast a vote in America until she was 31. But I can tell you, as much as she loves her roots and loves her heritage, I have met few people who love America as much as she does. Teresa is not alone. From soldiers to students, there are thousands of immigrants who have come to our shores and made America a better place.

Every year, hundreds seeking only a better life die in the desert. Millions labor in the shadows of our country, in fear and often abused. This does not serve our economy or our security. It doesn't reflect our values as a country built by immigrants.

It is time to fulfill the promise of America, so that those who work hard and take responsibility can build a better life for themselves and their families. Good people who are living here, working hard and paying taxes should have a path to equal citizenship in the American community. And families should be reunited more quickly. Our worker visa system should be fixed so it protects the wages and working conditions of U.S. workers and temporary workers. And as we do all this, we should improve our border security, fix our watch lists, and make Mexico a real partner, so that our country is safe from those who'd harm us.

A stronger America is also one that's respected in the world. But we will never be respected, unless, as Franklin Roosevelt once said, we are a good neighbor "who resolutely respects ... the rights of others."

Of course, Roosevelt was speaking of Latin America, and the message he sent has influenced every administration, from Kennedy to Clinton. They understood that a strong Latin America is key to a strong America.

The 1990s were particularly good for Latin America and U.S.-Latin American relations. There was an almost universal embrace of democracy and institutional reform—and Latin America edged ever closer to first-world economies and values. And that was good for the United States. What happens in this hemisphere has a profound effect on Main Street, U.S.A.—from our jobs to healthcare, from immigration to schools. In the Americas, foreign policy and domestic policy blur into one. It's fair to say that nearly every corner of the United States feels the effects of our relations with our neighbors.

That's why it's been such a disappointment that this Administration has forgotten Roosevelt's good advice. Instead of being a good neighbor, the president has ignored a wide range of ills—including political and financial crises, runaway unemployment, and drug trafficking. And his one-note policy toward Latin America of one-size-fits-all trade agreements have stripped the respect and partnership that marked the Clinton years.

In 1994, President Clinton convened the Summit of the Americas—the first summit in a quarter-century. As president, I will build on that spirit and help forge a new and broader "Community of the Americas." A community where neighbors look after neighbors, recognizing that we all have a stake in each other's future.

At the core of this Community of the Americas will be the bottom-line defense of democracy and the rule of law. While democracy has moved forward in countries like Mexico, Brazil, and Chile, we can't sit by and watch as mob violence drives a president from office, like what happened in Bolivia or Argentina—or even encourage him to flee, as we did in Haiti. We will not welcome a government named by a military junta, as was the case in Venezuela. Strong democratic states with transparent rules and a broad respect for the rule of law are essential to alleviating poverty and inequality in the region. As president, I will strongly support democratic institutions, assist democracy where it is troubled, and promote democracy in Cuba.

I will create a Council for Democracy with distinguished international leaders who can work with the Organization of American States to resolve crises before order is threatened and blood is shed. I will also triple funding for the National Endowment for Democracy's programs that strengthen democracy in Latin America. And I will support the Social Investment and Development Fund for the Americas. This $500 million fund will promote public and private partnerships in the region, and give training and developmental assistance to startup companies.

I will also create a "North American Security Perimeter" to better facilitate the legitimate travel of law-abiding citizens and crack down on bad actors trying to enter the United States. By working closely with our border neighbors to coordinate our customs, immigration and law enforcement policies, we can better protect the region from terrorist threats.

Finally, we are also losing the hearts and minds of a generation of leaders in Latin America by making it harder for young people to get visas to study here. As president, I will triple the number of educational exchanges, and encourage colleges to give tuition waivers to foreign students in exchange for internships overseas for our students.

The Community of Americas is about working together toward shared goals. In the war on terror, in the war on poverty, in the war on drug smuggling, in our many common battles, we must look to our neighbors as partners, not as second-class citizens, so this can truly be the Century of the Americas.

When I was in Vietnam, I served on a small boat on the Mekong Delta with men who came from places as diverse as South Carolina and Iowa ... Arkansas and California.

We were literally all in the same boat—and we came together as one. No one asked us our politics. No one cared where we went to school or what our backgrounds were.

We were just a band of brothers who all fought under the same flag, and all prayed to the same God. Today, we're a little bit older, we're a little bit greyer. But we still know how to fight for our country. And what we're fighting for is an America where all of us are truly in the same boat.

We're not just Democrats or Republicans. We are Americans. We have to end the divisions in this country. We have to work together for the America we can become.

So, I ask for your help. Talk to your neighbors; talk to your friends. Enlist in our cause.

My friends, this is the most important election of our lifetime. And that's not something I'm telling you. That's something Americans have told me again and again.

In great movements for civil rights and equal rights and the environment, we have come together as one America to give life to our mighty dream.

So come together again and stand up for a great purpose—to make America stronger at home and respected in the world.

We're a country of the future; we're a country of optimists. We're the can-do people. And no one understands that more than America's Latinos. People who've come here to work hard, pay taxes, and raise their children. No one has a bigger stake in America's future. We just need to believe in ourselves.

Que America sea America. Para Todos.

Let America be America again.

Si se puede! Si se puede! Si se puede!

Thank you, and God bless you.

★

Excerpts from

"Restoring American Leadership"
Remarks of Senator John Edwards
at the Center for Strategic and International Studies

How America exercises its leadership will be key to how we meet the many challenges and opportunities before us: whether it's transforming our relationship with a changing Russia or China or a unifying Europe, helping African countries deal with their problems and realize their great potential, keeping countries like India and Pakistan at peace, or fighting diseases like AIDS that ravage societies.

But the first responsibility of any government is the safety and security of its citizens. I believe that, today, that responsibility imposes three challenges above all others: first, to eliminate the threat of chemical, biological, and nuclear weapons; second, to win the war on terrorism; and third, to promote democracy and freedom around the world, especially the Middle East.

I believe that the successful pursuit of these goals can only come through American leadership of the world— not American disregard for it. Leadership is one of those words that is used so often it sometimes loses its meaning. But sometime soon, if our men and women in uniform are sent in battle into Iraq, we will see very clearly what leadership means. Because if we lead properly, others will join us, adding moral and military strength to our cause, sharing the dangers of war and the burdens of peace that will follow. But if we fail to lead, we will bear those risks and costs alone.

American leadership is about more than our ability to dominate others. It is about convincing others that our power serves their interests as well as our own. We inspire others to stand with us when we show that we are willing to stand with them, to listen to them, to take their views and contributions into account instead of taking them for granted. Too often, this administration seems to confuse leadership with going it alone and engagement with the compromise of principle—but real leadership is about setting principles and rallying others around them.

That kind of leadership rallied the free world to contain the threat of communism and built the transatlantic alliance that won the Cold War. That kind of leadership under President Bush's father turned back Iraq's aggression against Kuwait, not just by force of arms but by force of argument that brought the world to our side. Under President Clinton, that kind of American leadership rallied the world to end ethnic cleansing in Bosnia and Kosovo. And it inspired the world when we dedicated ourselves, despite all the risks and frustrations, to bring peace to the Middle East.

Over half a century, that kind of American leadership created institutions like NATO; it earned us allies; it won us true and enduring friends. And when America was attacked on September 11th, the legacy of that leadership could be seen in the solidarity of friends in every part of the world.

How then is it that one year later, what could and should be the world's fight against terrorism and weapons of mass destruction is seen as our fight alone?

...The problem is that in word and deed, the administration frequently sends the message that others don't matter. It rightly demands that our allies back efforts vital to America's interests, but then shows disdain for cooperative endeavors and agreements important to theirs. Indeed, it often treats allies as an afterthought, gratuitously rubbing in its contempt with statements like the one Secretary Rumsfeld recently made in Europe, when he said it never even occurred to him to use NATO to aid the war in Afghanistan.

Instead of demonstrating "purpose without arrogance" as the president promised in his inaugural address, the administration's foreign policy projects the opposite: arrogance without purpose. We seem determined to act alone for the sake of acting alone, which may be the easy way to achieve our short-term ends, but will never result in long-term security.

Our greatest challenges require the active commitment of our friends, allies, partners, and in fact, the world. Unilateral action will not win the war against terrorism. It will not stop the spread of weapons of mass destruction.

It will not produce thriving new democracies from the wreckage of failed or crushed totalitarian regimes. And it certainly won't protect the global environment, win the fight against HIV/AIDS, or address the scourge of deep poverty around the world.

This doesn't mean we will never have differences with our friends and allies. We will. But what's important is how we resolve those differences—or agree not to. We should always stick to our principles, do our very best to bring others to our way of thinking, and remain committed to resolving disputes in a respectful way. Picking up and walking away is not an exercise of leadership—it is an abdication of it. A leader who has to go it alone is no longer leading anybody.

In that context, let me say a few things about the administration's so-called preemption doctrine. Let's begin here: if we believe the United States is about to be attacked, or faces an imminent threat, then we have an absolute right to protect ourselves. It's called self-defense—it isn't new; it isn't controversial; and it doesn't need a fancy new name.

But this administration did not just reassert our right to self-defense. That would have been fine, especially when our security requires us to act before terrorists strike. Instead, they asserted a new doctrine that suggests a uniquely American right to use force wherever and whenever we decide it's appropriate. Some in the administration seem to believe that military force can be used as first resort to meet our legitimate foreign policy goals. The result has been distracting and damaging.

At a time when we should be working to lead the world towards a solution on the specific problem of Iraq, it is completely counter-productive for the administration to pronounce a doctrine that is not only unnecessary to justify action, but that alienates most of our friends and makes it harder for countries to cooperate with us.

...We must make a genuine commitment to help build a democratic Iraq after the fall of Saddam. And let's be clear: a genuine commitment means a real commitment of time, resources, and yes, leadership. Democracy will not spring up by itself or overnight in a multi-ethnic, complicated, society that has suffered under one repressive regime after another for generations. The Iraqi people deserve and need our help to rebuild their lives and to create a prosperous, thriving, open society. All Iraqis—including Sunnis, Shia and Kurds—deserve to be represented.

This is not just a moral imperative. It is a security imperative. It is in America's national interest to help build an Iraq at peace with itself and its neighbors, because a democratic, tolerant and accountable Iraq will be a peaceful regional partner. And such an Iraq could serve as a model for the entire Arab world.

We know that military planning is in high gear, and that's good; but democracy planning needs to be in high gear as well. For example, we should be asking NATO now to start planning for a post-conflict peacekeeping role, and we need to start consulting with others now about sharing the financial burden of reconstruction.

...We must lead our allies to greater collaboration, we must lead our friends to greater vigilance, we must lead our partners to greater participation—and we must lead problem states into adherence with the international agreements and programs to prevent proliferation.

If we're serious about dealing with this problem once and for all—and if we want to prevent future threats like Iraq from arising—then the United States must see non-proliferation for what it is: a strategic imperative, vital to our national interests.

Unfortunately, the administration's policies have moved the U.S. in the opposite direction. So far, the administration has spent far more diplomatic energy to weaken international consensus against proliferation than it has to strengthen it. Since coming into office, the administration has blocked efforts to strengthen the Biological Weapons Convention and the Nuclear Non-Proliferation Treaty. In its 31-page National Security Strategy, there is only one paragraph that says anything about strengthening preventive measures like non-proliferation.

This gratuitous unilateralism is coupled with neglect of programs that will make America safer over the long-term. Right now, the administration spends four times more on developing missile defense than on supporting programs to safeguard nuclear weapons in the former Soviet Union. It spends five times more on programs to resume nuclear testing than it does to prevent nuclear weapons from spreading.

These are the wrong priorities at exactly the wrong moment. The world needs more U.S. leadership on these issues, not less. Just as the U.S. must lead a global coalition against Iraq, it must forge a global coalition against the larger threat from weapons of mass destruction.

We must address the most insidious threat posed by weapons of mass destruction, the threat posed by terrorists. We must do much more to support the many disarmament programs already in place to dismantle weapons and prevent access to weapons-grade materials in Russia and the former Soviet states; we must devote the maximum resources necessary to support cooperative threat reduction programs, including Nunn-Lugar.

...The first thing we need to do with regard to the war on terror is to recognize that, like the fight against weapons of mass destruction, it will never be won through unilateral American action. As powerful as we are, we cannot be everywhere and learn everything without cooperation from our friends and allies. Al Qaeda alone is known to operate in more than 60 countries. We need the cooperation of intelligence and law enforcement agencies around the world to cast a global net for terrorists, to infiltrate their cells, learn their plans, disrupt their operations, cut off their funds, and stop them cold.

Second, the Bush administration must rethink its visceral rejection of greater leadership in post-Taliban Afghanistan. Our military brilliantly routed the Taliban and disrupted al Qaeda. Since that time, the administration's leadership in helping to provide security and stability in Afghanistan has been sorely lacking.

As of now, the international peacekeeping force is still confined to the area around Kabul, leaving most of Afghanistan in lawless disarray. That is a mistake, and we will pay for it when the unguarded fields of chaos in Afghanistan produce the next Osama bin Laden.

To be fair, the administration's position on whether to expand the international security presence outside of Kabul has recently shifted from active opposition to simple indifference. But that obviously isn't good enough. The security needs in Afghanistan are urgent. I saw that first-hand when I visited Afghanistan earlier this year. And last month's assassination attempt against President Karzai only underscores this.

Since returning from Afghanistan, I have consistently called for a sustained international presence throughout the country to fill the security vacuum, promote stability, and create the conditions democracy needs to take root and flourish.

We cannot do this alone; indeed—and again—we should not. But American leadership and American engagement are necessary. We have the finest military in the world, and should be willing to put troops on the ground. But real leadership here does not have to mean a commitment of enormous additional American resources.

We should be prepared to do what we do best, such as logistical, communications and intelligence support, and we should make a serious effort to recruit a much larger international force to help keep the peace. We've proved that we have firepower. Now we must show that we have staying power.

Finally, we need to do a much better job defending our security here at home. Since September 11, Americans have recognized an extraordinary threat: a sophisticated, international terrorist organization that is at war with America and present within America. And we have realized that we must respond, and respond strongly.

To make America safe in this new era, we must be willing to do two things that Washington in general and this administration in particular don't like to do: first, be honest with ourselves about what hasn't worked, and second, have the courage to try a new approach that will. As we do those two things, we have to remember who we are, what our values are, and what we stand for as a country: liberty, democracy, the rule of law. We have to commit that our actions today make us strong now and will make our children proud in 50 years.

...I believe we must do more to guarantee our safety. But when we limit our basic liberty, we should be able to explain why that's necessary to make us safer. That is a simple principle regularly ignored by this Attorney General.

On the detention of enemy combatants, for example, I believe the administration's approach is just plain wrong.

As a matter of law and a matter of common sense, a member of al Qaeda is not entitled to all the protections of our criminal justice system. Al Qaeda is at war with us, and we are at war with them.

But this administration is not simply saying that. They are saying that the government can arrest an American citizen on American soil, deny him access to a lawyer, deny him meaningful access to a judge, and keep him in jail for as long as they want. In other words, they are saying that they have the power to place certain U.S. citizens beyond due process of law, beyond any protection of law.

This is how they do things in dictatorships like Syria and Burma. This is not how we do things in America. But now, because of what this administration is doing, other countries can mimic our arguments to justify practices we have long condemned. In August, Liberia's Charles Taylor labeled three of his jailed critics as "illegal combatants" beyond the reach of civil courts. America should be a model for the world, but not this way.

...This administration would have us believe that we have to choose between security and freedom, even as they let us down on both scores. But the great thing about America is that we are strong and free.

That is what we ought to remember today—especially because our strength and freedom at home is an indispensable part of America's leadership to promote democracy and liberty around the world. The president's National Security Strategy is right to address that goal. But it is not enough to encourage other countries to protect basic rights unless we support those rights with vigorous action.

...The United States should lead a global coalition to promote democracy. I say that knowing full well that some of our partners in the war on terrorism are not democracies. But that is a contradiction we will have to confront. Countries like Egypt, Saudi Arabia and Uzbekistan aren't helping us in the long run if they keep denying their people peaceful avenues for expressing dissent. They're just driving their people toward violent alternatives.

Ultimately, there is no greater force for peace, prosperity, and against terrorism than the promotion of democratic regimes that respect human rights and the rule of law, both within and beyond their borders. That's one reason why the administration's lack of leadership planning for post-Saddam Iraq and lack of leadership action in post-Taliban Afghanistan are so troubling for our long-term security interests.

Today, the majority of people in the world choose their governments in democratic elections. But many of the newest democracies are losing popular support, in part because they have been unable to deliver on promises to end corruption and fight poverty. By the same token, many of the poorest countries of the world have been unable to escape the trap of underdevelopment, precisely because they have been unwilling to embrace democracy and good government.

We should therefore launch a far-reaching new effort to build the infrastructure of just and lawful societies—a free press and civil society, open and fair elections, and the legal, political, and regulatory institutions to make government accountable before the law and the people, and create a healthy environment for investment.

This requires more money for democratic assistance. It also requires a new approach to foreign aid. I support the administration's effort to allocate more money to those countries that govern justly and responsibly.

The effort to promote democracy has also stalled at the borders of the Islamic world. No area of the world is more critical to our interests, yet no area of the world is as undemocratic. We have tolerated and in fact supported authoritarian regimes in part because we depend on them for the oil our country needs. This is why a real commitment to energy independence—a commitment this administration lacks—will not only strengthen our own economy, but will also free us to promote the values we believe in.

...In short, we must forge a common approach with our closest allies to give the people of the Greater Middle East the same opportunities we all seek: to live with dignity and liberty; to live with hope and without fear; to live with opportunity and freedom.

We shouldn't pretend that this will be easy. Political change will take time and will have to come primarily from within. But it probably won't come at all unless attitudes about America and its intentions also change. In this respect, a visible American effort to help democracy take root in Iraq and Afghanistan will help.

So will rededicating ourselves to ending the Israeli-Palestinian conflict. We must remember this fundamental fact: America's power makes it unique; but its principles and authority make it great. And our greatness comes through the exercise of principled leadership— leadership that sets an example, leadership that inspires others to follow; leadership that will make others stronger and bring more countries by our side. It is the kind of leadership that presidents of both political parties understood and practiced. It is the kind of leadership we need today.

★

Excerpts from

"Protecting the Homeland"
Remarks of Senator John Edwards
at the Brookings Institution

...The first and foremost responsibility of any government is to protect its citizens from harm. It is time for all of us, without regard to party, to say what everyone of us knows: Washington is not doing enough to make America safe. If the administration continues to do too little, it will be too late again. We must do better.

I don't accept the notion that another devastating attack is inevitable. I will never accept that. It's fearful, it's defeatist, and it's a victory for the terrorists. Our job is to do everything we can to stop them. We have to summon every last bit of American strength, guts, and wits to win this war. If we do, we will.

Protecting America requires clear leadership from America around the world, and a comprehensive homeland defense here at home. Today I'm going to focus on what we need to do to strengthen our domestic security, offensively to catch terrorists before they attack, and defensively to prevent harm if an attack comes.

...When it comes to fighting the war on terror around the globe, we have to keep the big picture in mind, and stay true to our principles. This administration needs to rethink its visceral, short-sighted rejection of greater leadership in post-Taliban Afghanistan. We need a new relationship with Saudi Arabia, one that no longer ignores that regime's pattern of tolerance and denial when it comes to terrorists. We need to address the grave proliferation risk posed by North Korea, and we need to do it in a way that is clear, competent, and consistent.

...First and foremost, there simply is no comprehensive strategy for domestic security. We've addressed a few vulnerabilities, not the full range of challenges. Yes, we've created a massive new federal agency, and it's a positive step that I supported. But at this point the new Department of Homeland Security is more of a political achievement for the administration than a substantive achievement for America's security. A new agency and new office space won't help us infiltrate terrorist organizations operating right now in our country. It won't stop terrorists or their weapons from getting through the holes in our borders or our ports. It won't provide equipment and training for police to protect bridges and tunnels, or cause companies to protect vulnerable chemical plants. It won't help police officers, firemen, and EMT's on the front lines to coordinate their response in the event of an attack. In short, the homeland security bill is a perfect example of how long it takes Washington to come up with an answer that won't even solve the problem.

Second, this administration continues to have its priorities out of whack. Against all reason, the administration stubbornly clings to tax cuts that will benefit only the top one percent of Americans while arguing that we can't afford vital measures to protect the very lives of our people. Congress has passed legislation to strengthen border security, port security, cybersecurity, and guard against bioterrorism. I wrote provisions in all those bills, but for the most part they're not being funded the way they should be. President Bush has actually vetoed billions of dollars for domestic defense, and he is refusing to release $1.5 billion that should go to police, firefighters, and first responders who face layoffs as I speak.

The president made a big show out of vetoing a $5 billion emergency bill, half of which was for domestic defense, while the rest included money to fight forest fires and essential aid for Israel. But $5 billion is about what it will cost for just one month if we fully eliminate the estate tax under the president's plan, mostly benefiting just 3,000 or so multi-millionaire families. How this administration can prefer tax cuts for the most fortunate one percent of Americans over domestic defense for 100 percent of Americans is beyond me, but they do.

...In short, when it comes to homeland security, the administration has been expert at politics and erratic in practice. Instead, homeland security should be our unequivocal priority; our strategy must be comprehensive; and our approach must honor the way of life we are defending: faith and family, duty and service, individual freedoms and a common purpose to build one nation under God.

....September 11th awakened us to the massive damage terrorists could cause with airplanes, and we've taken good measures to harden airline security. Unfortunately, we have a dangerous pattern of closing the barn door after the terrorists have attacked. It's time to get ahead of them. We know they want to cause the most death, destruction, economic disruption, and fear they can. And so while we can never predict just what terrorists will do, we have a pretty good sense about other likely targets. We need to harden those targets.

Start with nuclear safety. Today, nuclear waste shipments are highly vulnerable—we need better security for the routes and stronger casks for the shipments. The situation at nuclear plants is even more troubling. Before 9/11, plants were failing about half their security evaluations. Even now, guards have repeatedly reported that they don't have essential training and equipment, and they're understaffed and underpaid.

These are the very same issues we saw in airport security prior to 9/11. And we know how we met that problem, even if the administration wasn't crazy about it. We did it by putting well-trained, well-paid federal guards into airports. Airport security isn't perfect, but it's a whole lot better than before. Given the terrible cost of an attack on a nuclear plant or a theft from one, we need a federal security force for nuclear facilities, carefully trained and regularly tested through emergency simulations.

America's 12,000 chemical facilities also pose a dangerous threat. There are roughly 25,000 fires, spills or explosions involving hazardous materials every year. The Union Carbide chemical disaster in India killed at least 3,000 people—and it was an accident. An attack could achieve horrifying results. One hundred and twenty three plants store toxic chemicals that could endanger a million people or more if they were released.

The Bush administration was actually moving towards a commonsense solution that would set minimum standards for safety at chemical plants—internal EPA documents clearly indicate that administration officials consider this a grave threat. But dangerously true to form, after lobbying by the chemical industry, the administration abandoned that approach.

Once again, corporate special interests have trumped the interests of ordinary Americans—in this case, with potentially devastating consequences.

...I believe we should do whatever it takes for domestic defense. At the same time, as I've said many times before, our economic security requires a deliberate return to fiscal discipline. In short, we should strengthen our domestic defense, and we should pay for the steps to do it. We can and must do both.

...Strengthening our domestic defense is a challenge, but Americans have always risen to great challenges. There is no cause greater or nobler than protecting the country we love from the challenges we face. I believe we can do it, and we will do it if we are determined and if we work together.

★

Excerpts from

"Strategy of Prevention, Not Preemption"

Remarks of Senator John Edwards
at Des Moines Public Schools Central Campus

Foreign policy, just like domestic policy, is about improving people's lives. It is about expanding opportunity. The opportunity to make America stronger, safer, and more secure. And the opportunity to stand for values like tolerance, freedom, and democracy around the world.

...As I travel around our country, I know that you are worried about the threats posed by terrorists who have attacked us on our own soil and threaten to do so again. You are concerned about the possibility that our enemies will gain access to weapons of mass murder and use them. You are upset that American policies are opposed and resented in many parts of the world even among longtime friends. You want to know how we can restore respect for America overseas; and how we can persuade others to stand with us to meet the most fundamental challenges we face.

...During the Cold War, these weapons were primarily a problem for the major military powers, to handle through maintaining deterrence; arms control negotiations and superpower summits. But today, we face a terrorist movement that has no interest in bargaining, only in killing. If al Qaeda had possessed a nuclear, chemical or biological weapon on September 11th, there is no doubt in my mind they would have tried to use it. That is why to win the global war on terror, America does not need a new doctrine of pre-emption; we need a new strategy of prevention.

We face an increased threat from hostile governments in countries like North Korea and Iran. Time and technology have enabled both to take steps toward the development of nuclear arms; and North Korea may already have succeeded. These states and others also have the capacity to produce and sell dangerous technologies to terrorists intent on doing us harm. At the same time, the source materials for producing weapons of mass destruction have become vulnerable to theft or black market sale, particularly in the former Soviet Union.

Meanwhile, the international rules and institutions we rely on to stymie and isolate wrong-doers are riddled with loopholes and gaps. The Bush administration has responded by pretending that these rules and institutions do not matter. I say they do matter, and that the right policy is not to ignore them, but to fix them.

But has this administration taken any common sense steps to secure these weapons? Have we provided adequate funding for programs to stop their spread? Have we worked every angle to stop North Korea's and Iran's nuclear programs? Have we put our weight behind strengthening the Biological Weapons Convention? Did we support the Comprehensive Nuclear Test Ban Treaty? The answer to each question is no.

This administration's approach to protecting America from weapons of mass destruction can be summed up simply: wait until our enemies gather strength, and then use force to stop them. We should be exercising every option we have to stop the spread of deadly weapons before war becomes our only option.

...The threat we face is obvious.... It requires action on multiple fronts in dozens of countries. It demands that we use every tool in our national security arsenal— deploying foreign aid, engaging multilateral institutions, conducting diplomacy, applying sanctions, threatening and sometimes using force.

It requires sustained, consistent leadership—leadership that we have not had from this administration. And it will require a lot more than simply getting rid of one Middle Eastern dictator. ...A one-dimensional foreign policy for a three-dimensional world will not secure our nation. And without our long-standing allies by our side, we cannot stop proliferation at the source. We need them to shut down smuggling networks, enforce international rules, support economic sanctions, and stand with us should force become necessary. We need more than coalitions of the willing; we need coalitions of the able.

...[We] must lead in a way that brings others to us so that we can protect America from the threat of weapons of mass destruction. So we can succeed in Iraq and Afghanistan. So we can win the war against terrorism.

And so we can help foster democracy and freedom and human rights throughout the Middle East and the world.

...Because you can't promote freedom without the support of free countries around the world. You can't promote freedom if you're not respected by the dissidents and democrats who are struggling to be free. Right now democrats in the Arab world simply do not see the U.S. as a credible champion of their cause. They know the Bush administration itself has set a miserable example on civil liberties and human rights here at home; they have seen us abandon America's traditional role as a peace-maker in the Middle East.

...We can employ our influence but we cannot impose our vision. And to employ our influence, we need to restore respect for America in the Middle East and around the world; we need to regain our capacity for leadership. There is no question that America is a military power this world has never seen. And I will keep our military strong—with the resources to do its job—and treat America's military men and women with the support and respect they've earned.

But leadership isn't just military power and strength. It's about convincing others that fighting terrorism and defending freedom is right. That fighting poverty and preventing the spread of HIV/AIDS are efforts the world should undertake together. This does not mean that the international institutions and alliances that served America's interests so well for decades are perfect. They're not. But rather than disregard or undermine them, we should lead the effort to make our alliances better and relevant for the threats we now face.

President Clinton realized this when he transformed NATO into an alliance of the 21st Century with new members and new missions. NATO is now in command of the security force in Afghanistan—and I believe that we should turn to NATO for help in Iraq.

...To meet these global challenges, it will take hard work, sacrifice, and courage. All of these steps I will begin as your president. I plan to accomplish as much as I can, but this common cause will continue for years to come. And the young people here today will carry on our efforts. They will do so with humility, not arrogance, with intelligence, not ideology, and with their energy to enrich the quality of life in our country and around the world.

★

Excerpts from

"Two Americas"
Remarks of Senator John Edwards

This election is about more than ending the Bush administration; it's about a new beginning for America. And we have so much work to do. Because the truth is, we still live in two different Americas: one for the privileged few who get what they want, whenever they want it, and another one for everybody else. It doesn't have to be this way. We can change this country. We can build one America.

We still have two health care systems in this country: one for families that get the best health care money can buy, and one for everybody else given out by insurance companies, drug companies and HMOs. Millions of Americans have no health care coverage at all. It doesn't have to be this way.

We can cover every child and provide parents with a tax credit to cover this cost for doing the right thing. We can cover our most vulnerable adults. And we can finally stand up to those drug companies, insurance companies and HMO's and say join our efforts to cut costs or we will end your wasteful ways for you. We can do this, yes we can.

We shouldn't have two public school systems, one for the most affluent communities, one for everybody else. You and I do not believe that the quality of a child's education should be controlled by the affluence of the community they live in

We can build one school system that educates every child by ending the damage being done and fully funding, fixing, and changing "No Child Left behind." We also have to pay teachers more and provide incentives so they teach in the places that need them the most.

We shouldn't have two tax systems in this country: one for the special interests and the big corporations, many of whom pay no taxes at all. And one for you. Right? Folks who just work hard, pay your taxes. You're carrying the tax burden in this country. You know that. It shouldn't be that way.

This president wants to shift the tax burden from wealth onto work—cutting or eliminating dividends taxes, capital gains taxes, estate taxes for even the wealthiest estates. In his America, a public school teacher pays a higher tax rate on their work than a millionaire stockbroker pays on their unearned wealth.

This is wrong. It is wrong for our values. It is also wrong for our economy. The economic engine of our economy are the millions of Americans who work hard in every corner of this great city and every corner of our great country.

The way to grow the economy is to grow and strengthen the middle class. The way a rich nation gets richer is by giving all its citizens the chance to succeed, not by only helping those like me who've already succeeded beyond our wildest dreams.

We need to fix our tax code to reward work, not wealth, and to give middle-class families a chance to save again. It isn't enough to roll back the Bush tax cuts—we need a new approach to taxes that puts our tax code back in line with our values and gives middle-class families a chance for some security again.

I also want to say a word about an issue that's important to me personally. I think it's important for the country. You never hear pundits and politicians talk about it anymore: 35 million Americans who live in poverty every single day.

There are millions of Americans working fulltime and living in poverty. And here's the reason we should not just talk about but do something about millions of Americans who live in poverty, because it is wrong. We have a moral responsibility to lift those families out of poverty. You and I together can do this in a country of our wealth. That's what we believe in.

It's what the Democratic Party believes in. We need to stand up for these families. In a country of our wealth and prosperity, to have children going to bed hungry, to have children who don't have clothes to keep them warm, to have millions of Americans who work full-time every day working for minimum wage and living in poverty is wrong.

Let me tell you what we're going to do. We're going to build an America where we say no to kids going to bed hungry, no to kids who don't have the clothes to keep them warm and no forever to any American working full-time and living in poverty. Not in our America, not in the America that you and I are going to build together. You and I can do something about that. This is the America we believe in!

We still have two governments in America: one for the insiders, the lobbyists, and the special interests, and then whatever is leftover is for you.

But in the America you and I build together, we will have one government that works for you—not those insiders, not those lobbyists, not those special interests but you. All you have to do is look at that Medicare prescription drug bill.

Here we go again. Millions of seniors desperately need prescription drugs, and look at what we've got. We've got a bill with billions of dollars in your money that goes to HMOs instead of seniors. We're driving seniors out of Medicare into HMOs. Every provision that could have been used to bring down the cost of prescription drugs: using the power of the government to negotiate a better price, allowing prescription drugs into this country from Canada, and doing something finally about these drug company ads on television that are completely out of control.

Every one of those things would have brought down the cost of prescription drugs for America's seniors, but the drug companies were against them so they all came out. Let me say this in very simple language that every-body will understand.

This democracy does not belong to them. We ought to stop this revolving door in and out of the government to these high-priced lobbying firms. We ought to shine a bright light on what these lobbyists are doing, know what they're doing, who they're lobbying for and what money is being spent. I have never taken a dime from a Washington lobbyist and I never will.

And one other thing we ought to do is stop this war profiteering going on in Iraq each and every single day.

I haven't spent my whole life in politics and most people view that as a good thing. But I have spent enough time in Washington to know how much we need to change things. The lobbyists and the politicians and the insiders are so stuck in their system and making things work for themselves—they forget about your needs. Well, we remember and we are going to change this.

We also live in a country that in far too many ways, it still divided by race. This is something I've lived with my entire life. I grew up in the South in the '50s and '60s.

From the time I was very young, I saw the ugly face of segregation and discrimination. I saw young African-American kids shuffled upstairs in movie theaters. I saw white only signs on restaurant doors and luncheon counters. When I was in the sixth grade, my teacher walked into the classroom to tell us that the school was about to be integrated and he wouldn't teach any longer because he wouldn't teach in an integrated school. I feel such an enormous personal responsibility when it comes to issues of race and equality and civil rights and we have so much work to do in America.

For economic equality, for educational equality, standing up for judges that we know with a certainty will enforce the civil rights laws. That is why it is so important to continue the march forward on civil rights in America

And I want to say one other thing about this. I have heard some discussion, and debate, among pundits and some politicians about where, and in front of what audiences we should talk about race, equality and civil rights. I'll tell you where we should talk about it—everywhere. This is not an African American issue, not an Hispanic American issue, not an Asian American issue, this is an American issue.

The truth is that we want our children and grandchildren to be the first generation to grow up in an America that's no longer divided by race.

It's what our values are. What we believe in. It's what kind of country we want our children and grandchildren to grow up in. We have to stand up, you and I, together. We have to stand up for equality, for freedom, for civil rights. We can do this together, yes, we can.

We've also had two different images of America over the last 40 years. There's the image of America we are proud of, right? America, this great shining light, this beacon of freedom, democracy and human rights that everyone looked up to. And now the image that George Bush has given us. America acting on its own, unilaterally, disrespecting the rest of the world. It doesn't have to be that way.

You and I can build an image of America around the world where we're once again looked up to and respected. The truth is every child, every family in America will be safer and more secure if they grow up in a world where we're once again looked up to and respected. That's the world you and I can create together.

And to those people who say to me it's been this way too long, you can't change it. This is what I say. Cynics didn't build America; optimists built America. You and I can do this together.

By the way, if I can just be personal about this for a minute, I've been listening to this kind of pessimism my whole life. When I was young, I decided I wanted to be a lawyer. Everybody said, now, wait a minute, wait a minute.

Your father works in the mill. Nobody in your family's ever been to college and you're talking about being a lawyer?

Then when I finally was lucky enough to become a lawyer, I would go into courtrooms, representing families just like yours.

We'd be on one side of the courtroom and on the other side of the courtroom would be all the armies of lawyers representing the big corporations. And you know, they always had the best lawyers money can buy—very experienced, very distinguished. And they would look across the courtroom and pull on their coats like this and say "what is he doing here? He thinks he belongs in the same courtroom with us?"

Well, here's what happened. I beat them and then I beat them again and I beat them again. I'm proud of those fights on behalf of you and families just like yours.

And then I ran for the senate. Here we go, same thing again. We have an incumbent republican senator, hand picked by Jesse Helms—part of the Helms political machine in North Carolina.

Everybody said that young fella thinks he's going to take on the Helms political machine in North Carolina, who does he think he is. Here's what happened. I took on the Helms political machine, beat that incumbent republican senator and now I'm the senior senator from North Carolina, not Jesse Helms and that's a good thing for America.

I'm just glad that you are having as much fun as I am. That's all I can say. Think about this in your own mind. Every one of you knows exactly what I'm talking about. Just think in your own mind, how many times has somebody said to you, you can't do this. Right? You know what I'm saying.

You know exactly what I'm talking about. So when we hear those same voices telling us we can't win this election—that you and I can't change America. I say just watch us.

You and I can do this together. I can't do it by myself. But I know that you and I can do it together. We can make this country one that we're all proud of one, that works for everybody.

But I want to say one other thing. If you have been watching the presidential debate over the last couple of months, one of the things you've seen is some of the other candidates attacking each other.

You know, it's sort of so and so said this or did this last week or two weeks ago or five years ago or ten years ago. Well, let me be very direct with everybody here about something. If you're looking for the candidate that's going to do the best job of attacking the other Democrats, that's not me.

The American people are going to reject the tired old negative politics of the past. This election is bigger than that. This election is about lifting up the American people. It's about the future of America. It's about making the American people believe again that everything is possible. Our campaign is not based on the politics of cynicism. It's based on the politics of hope, the politics of what's possible.

The truth is, this country has been here before. 70 years ago, Franklin Roosevelt came into office at one of the worst times in American history. He believed that everything was possible. He lifted up the American people and look, we have social security today as a result.

John Kennedy came into office at one of the worst times of racial division in American history. He believed that everything was possible, and he gave the American people what they were hungry for—hope.

What we believe—what I believe—is that you should never look down on anybody, that we should lift people up. We don't believe in tearing people apart. We believe in bringing people together. We believe, I believe, that the family you're born into and the color of your skin in our America should never control what you are able to do.

Join this campaign. Join this cause to build one America. You and I can do this together. Thank you all very much.

★

Biography of John Kerry

John F. Kerry was born on December 11, 1943 at Fitzsimons Army Hospital in Colorado. His father, Richard, volunteered in the Army Air Corps and flew DC-3's and B-29's as a test pilot during World War II. His mother, Rosemary, was a lifelong community activist and devoted parent. She was a Girl Scout leader for fifty years, and one of her proudest possessions was her fifty-year Girl Scout pin. She was an environmentalist and a community activist.

Not long after John Kerry was born, the family settled in Massachusetts. Growing up there, his parents taught him the values of service and responsibility and the blessings of his Catholic faith, lessons John Kerry carries with him to this day.

Because his father was a Foreign Service Officer in the Eisenhower administration, John Kerry traveled a lot when he was young. On these trips, he learned firsthand what makes America a leader in the world—our optimism and our democratic values. And he learned that nations across the world share many common goals and that the best way to achieve them is through building strong alliances.

As he was graduating from Yale, John Kerry volunteered to serve in Vietnam, because, as he later said, "It was the right thing to do." He believed that "to whom much is given, much is required." And he felt he had an obligation to give something back to his country. John Kerry served two tours of duty. On his second tour, he volunteered to serve on a Swift Boat in the river deltas, one of the most dangerous assignments of the war. His leadership, courage, and sacrifice earned him a Silver Star, a Bronze Star with Combat V, and three Purple Hearts.

But John Kerry's wartime experience taught him a painful lesson that he could not forget, even after he returned home. In the midst of battle, he had seen the lives of his fellow soldiers, his friends, put at risk because some leaders in Washington were making bad decisions. He decided he had a responsibility to his friends still serving, the friends he had lost, and his country, to help restore responsible leadership in America.

So he decided to become active as a Vietnam Veteran Against the War (VVAW). He became a spokesman for VVAW and later co-founded Vietnam Veterans of America. Only twenty-seven years old, John Kerry sounded this call to reason in April 1971 when he testified before the Senate Foreign Relations Committee and posed the powerful question, "How do you ask a man to be the last man to die for a mistake?"

Later, John Kerry accepted another tour of duty—to serve in America's communities. After graduating from Boston College Law School in 1976, John Kerry went to work as a top prosecutor in Middlesex County, Massachusetts. He took on organized crime and put behind bars "one of the state's most notorious gangsters, the number two organized crime figure in New England." He fought for victims' rights and created programs for rape counseling.

John Kerry was elected Lieutenant Governor in 1982. In that office, he organized the nation's Governors to combat the acid rain that was polluting lakes, rivers, and the nation's water supply. Two years later, he was elected to the United States Senate and he has won reelection three times since. He is now serving his fourth term, after winning again in 2002.

John Kerry entered the Senate with a reputation as a man of conviction. He confirmed that reputation by taking bold decisions on important issues. He helped provide health insurance for millions of low-income children. He has fought to improve public education, protect our natural environment, and strengthen our economy. He has been praised as one of the leading environmentalists in the Senate, who stopped the Bush-Cheney plan to drill in the Arctic National Wildlife Refuge.

John Kerry has never forgotten the lessons he learned as a young man-lessons that have been strengthened in his nineteen years on the Senate Foreign Relations

Committee. He has learned that America must work with other countries to achieve our goals and the world's common goals. From his ground-breaking work on the Iran-Contra scandal to his leadership on global AIDS, John Kerry has distinguished himself as one of our nation's most respected voices on national security and international affairs.

As chairman of the Senate Select Committee on POW/MIA Affairs, he worked closely with John McCain to learn the truth about American soldiers missing in Vietnam and to normalize relations with that country. As the ranking Democrat on the East Asian and Pacific Affairs Subcommittee, he is a leading expert on that region, including North Korea.

Years before September 11th, John Kerry wrote *The New War*, an in-depth study of America's national security in the 21st Century. He worked on a bipartisan basis to craft the American response to September 11th and has been a leading voice on American policy in Iraq and Afghanistan, the war on terrorism, the Middle East peace process and Israel's security.

John Kerry would not be running today if it were not for the enthusiastic support of his family. He is married to Teresa Heinz Kerry, and they have a blended family that includes two daughters, three sons, one grandchild, and a German Shepard named Cym.

★

Biography of John Edwards

John Edwards was born in Seneca, South Carolina and raised in Robbins, North Carolina. There John learned the values of hard work and perseverance from his father, Wallace, who worked in the textile mills for thirty-six years, and from his mother, Bobbie, who ran a shop and worked at the post office. Working alongside his father at the mill, John developed his strong belief that all Americans deserve an equal opportunity to succeed and be heard.

A proud product of public schools, John became the first person in his family to attend college. He worked his way through North Carolina State University where he graduated with high honors in 1974, and then earned a law degree with honors in 1977 from the University of North Carolina at Chapel Hill.

For the next twenty years, John dedicated his career

to representing families and children hurt by the indifference and negligence of others. Standing up against the powerful insurance industry and their armies of lawyers, John helped these families through the darkest moments of their lives to overcome tremendous challenges. His passionate advocacy for people like the ones who worked in the mill with his father earned him respect and recognition across the country.

In 1998, John took this commitment into politics to give a voice in the United States Senate to the people he had represented throughout his career. He ran for the Senate and won, defeating an incumbent Senator.

In Congress, John is championing the issues that matter to American families. He is working to provide Americans with quality health care and he co-authored the Patients' Bill of Rights and helped pass it in the Senate. He fought for middle-class tax cuts to help families save and get ahead. And he worked to improve our schools, fund No Child Left Behind, improve teacher pay, and expand after-school programs.

Senator Edwards is working every day to protect our civil liberties and our rights: standing up to radical judicial appointees like Judge Pickering. He is standing up to the big polluters to preserve our environment and keep our air and our water clean. And he has called for fiscal discipline to cut the deficit in half to save Social Security and Medicare, and offered real reforms to change the way campaigns are financed.

As a member of the Select Committee on Intelligence, Senator Edwards has worked tirelessly for a strong national defense and to strengthen the security of our homeland. In the wake of September 11th, he served as a member of the joint House and Senate panel investigating the terrorist attacks.

John Edwards has been a leader in fighting bioterrorism, and he's taken on powerful special interests to safeguard our nuclear power plants and chemical plants. He was one of the first to call for fundamental reforms in the way our intelligence agencies are organized to catch terrorists here at home and around the world. And he was one of the first to travel to Afghanistan to visit our troops after they defeated the Taliban.

As the Senator from North Carolina, John Edwards represents the world's largest army installation complex as well as the headquarters of the Marine Antiterrorism Task Force. He has been active in strengthening our military and improving the lives of our men and women in uniform and their families. He has proposed to extend tax exemptions for military personnel in combat zones and provide National Guard families with financial help paying for child care in their home town.

Senator Edwards and his wife, Elizabeth, whom he met when both were law students at Chapel Hill, were married in 1977. They have had four children, including: their eldest daughter, Catharine, a recent graduate of Princeton University; six-year-old Emma Claire, and a four-year-old son, Jack. Their first child, Wade, died in 1996.

Senator Edwards and Elizabeth opened the Wade Edwards Learning Lab in Raleigh, North Carolina. The learning lab offers students after-school access to computers and tutoring in technology. The Edwards also established an education foundation in memory of their son that offers college scholarships to students.

★

Credits:

DESIGN BY:

Polina Pinchevsky, NANA Design

PHOTOGRAPHS BY:

Lou Dematteis, Sharon Farmer, Getty Images, Michael Nemec

PRODUCTION BY:

Mary E. Argodale

PRODUCTION MANAGEMENT BY:

Sonita M. Saluja-Herath